ENGLISH AS A SECOND LANGUAGE — Secondary Cycle Two ■ Year Two — Grammar Activities

CONNECTING
THROUGH ENGLISH

Grammar

BRUNO GATTUSO ■ ALEXANDRA PASIAN
Coordinator: Lilianne Bohémier

Centre de ressources de la Faculté d'éducation
Université d'Ottawa - University of Ottawa
Faculty of Education Resource Centre

Éditions Grand Duc
Groupe Éducalivres inc.
955, rue Bergar, Laval (Québec) H7L 4Z6
Téléphone : 514 334-8466 ■ Télécopie : 514 334-8387
InfoService : 1 800 567-3671

ACKNOWLEDGEMENTS

The publisher wishes to thank the following people for their participation in the writing of some chapter:

Mr. Mark Rozahegy
Ms. Judith Rohlf
Ms. Maria-Lee Arpino

The publisher wishes to thank the following people for their comments and suggestions during the development of this project:

Mr. Alain Bissonnette, École Édouard-Montpetit, Commission scolaire de Montréal
Ms. Annie Clément, École Félix-Leclerc, Comission scolaire des Affluents
Ms. Annie Dumay, École Père-Marquette, Commission scolaire de Montréal
Mr. Jean-François Duquette, École Cité des Jeunes, Commission scolaire des Trois-Lacs
Ms. Louise Simard, École Louis-Cyr, Commission scolaire des Grandes-Seigneuries

ILLUSTRATIONS: Volta Création

Connecting Through English
Grammar

© 2008, Éditions Grand Duc, A division of Groupe Éducalivres Inc.
955 Bergar Street, Laval (Québec) H7L 4Z6
Telephone: 514 334-8466 ■ Fax: 514 334-8387 ■ www.grandduc.com
All rights reserved.

We acknowledge the financial support of the Government of Canada through the Book Publishing Industry Development Program (BPIDP) for our publishing activities.

It is illegal to reproduce this publication, in full or in part, in any form or by any means (electronic, mechanical, photographic, recording, magnetic or other) without first obtaining written permission from the publisher. By respecting this request, you will encourage the authors in the pursuit of their careers.

PRODUCT CODE 3760
ISBN 978-2-7655-0264-7

Legal deposit
Bibliothèque et Archives nationales du Québec, 2008
Library and Archives Canada, 2008

Printed in Canada
1 2 3 4 5 6 7 8 9 0 S 7 6 5 4 3 2 1 0 9 8

Contents

▶▶ **Letter to Students** 1

Unit 1   AT ALL COSTS

Nouns and Articles 2
- Nouns
- The Plural Form of Nouns
- Articles
- Quantifiers with Count and Non-count Nouns

Pronouns and Possessive Adjectives 6
- Personal Pronouns
- Possessive Adjectives, Possessive Pronouns and Reflexive Pronouns
- Indefinite Pronouns
- Demonstrative Pronouns
- There Is/There Are

Simple Verb Tenses 16
- The Simple Present Tense
- The Simple Past Tense
- The Simple Future Tense

Wrap-up 29

Unit 2   TUNING IN

Adverbs 34
- Adverbs of Frequency
- Adverbs of Time
- Adverbs of Manner
- Adverbs of Intensity or Degree

Prepositions 40
- Prepositions of Time
- Prepositions of Location and Direction
- Prepositions of Manner

Continuous Verb Tenses 44
- The Present Continuous Tense
- The Past Continuous Tense

Wrap-up 48

Unit 3   ON THE EDGE

Punctuation 50
- Punctuation Marks (Period, exclamation mark, question mark, apostrophe, hyphen)
- More Punctuation Marks (Comma, colon, semi-colon)
- Quotation Marks

Perfect and Conditional Verb Tenses 56
- The Present Perfect Tense
- Choosing Between the Simple Past and the Present Perfect
- The Past Perfect Tense
- The Conditional Tense
- The Sequence of Verb Tenses

Wrap-up 68

Unit 4 — Mirror, Mirror…
- Modal Auxiliaries 72
- The Conditional Tense + an "If-clause" 82
- Wrap-up 85

Unit 5 — Nothing but the Truth
- Adjectives: Comparatives and Superlatives 88
- Question Tags 91
- Figures of Speech 92
- Wrap-up 96

Unit 6 — Beyond Reality
- Direct and Indirect Speech 98
- Active and Passive Voice 100
- The Past Unreal Conditional 102
- Confusables — Homonyms and Vocabulary Building 106
- Wrap-up 108

Unit 7 — Wondering About Wonders
- Placement of Adjectives 110
- Gerunds and Infinitives 112
- Phrasal Verbs 116
- Idiomatic Expressions 118
- Wrap-up 120

▶▶ Reference Section
- A. Capitalization 124
- B. Punctuation 126
- C. Table of Common Phrasal Verbs 128
- D. Idiomatic Expressions 130
- E. An Overview of Verb Tenses 132
- F. Table of Common Irregular Verbs 138

▶▶ Letter to Students

Montreal, September 1

Dear Students,

It's the start of a new year and another great adventure in English!

The *Connecting Through English* grammar activity book is specially designed to help you improve your English skills as autonomously as possible.

In this activity book, you will notice that there is continuity between the topics and issues covered in the *Connecting Through English* Student Book (Secondary Cycle Two, Year Two). This is because each unit has been structured to help you reinforce the notions introduced in the Student Book as well as practise with new material. In this way, you will continue to develop your vocabulary and your ESL competencies as well as gain confidence in using English.

Our goal is to help you learn English through meaningful tasks.
Give it your best shot. Have fun!

Sincerely,
The Team
Alexandra, Bruno and Lilianne

"*Learning English opens doors*... Connecting Through English *opens minds.*"

UNIT 1 — At All Costs

Nouns and Articles

① Do you know where this **year's race** will be held?

② I believe it's in **Montreal**. Why do you ask?

③ My **cousin's husband** wants to participate in **the race** and he wants to know where to register.

Tell him to send his **registration** to **the International Race Committee** and tell him to buy **a** good **pair** of running **shoes**.

Focus on...

Nouns

A noun refers to a person, place, thing, idea or quality. *Boy, park, pencil, music* and *happiness* are all nouns. Common nouns refer to things like objects, professions and locations, not names of people or places. They do not start with a capital letter.

Proper Nouns (names of specific persons, places or things)	
Proper nouns always start with a **capital letter**.	*Colombo, Africa, Andy Warhol, James A. Naismith, Antarctica, the Underground Railroad*
Possessive Nouns (nouns that show ownership)	
1. Possessive nouns are formed by adding **'s** to nouns in the singular.	• *Lisa's purse* • *the athlete's gear*
2. For plural nouns, an apostrophe (') is added.	• *the dogs' owners* • *the neighbours' car*
3. With words that end in an *s* sound, the possessive is formed by adding **'s** or just (').	• *the princess' crown or the princess's crown* • *Charles' car or Charles's car*
4. For pluralized family names, an apostrophe (') is added.	• *the Johnsons' canoe*

Practise!

Correct the nouns in the following paragraph.

A Day at the Boston Marathon

(francis) _____ lives in (san diego) _____ but comes to (montreal) _____ every year for the marathon. His friend (miguel) _____, who comes from (spain) _____, accompanies him every year. Recently, (miguel) _____ finished second at the (boston) _____ Marathon. (francis) _____ didn't complete the race because he twisted his ankle a few kilometres from the finish line. The medics took him to (dr.) _____ (hines) _____ clinic. The (doctors) _____ office is on the third floor. While waiting to see the doctor, he read a magazine article about the (pacific oceans) _____ deepest point – the (mariana trench) _____. It is not only the deepest point in the ocean, it is also (earths) _____ deepest point.

Focus on...

The Plural Form of Nouns

Here are nine general ways to make singular nouns plural:

Rule	Examples	Exceptions
1. For most nouns, add **s**.	car**s**, horse**s**, hat**s**	
2. If a noun ends with **s, ch, sh, x** or **z**, add **es**.	bus**es**, church**es**, bush**es**, tax**es**, quizz**es**	When **ch** sounds like a **k**, only add **s**. Example: stomach**s**
3. If a noun ends with **f** or **fe**, change the **f** to a **v** and add **es**.	scar**ves**, loa**ves**, lea**ves**, kni**ves**	belie**fs**, chie**fs**, clif**fs**, gul**fs**, proo**fs**, roo**fs**, sa**fes**
4. If a noun ends with **y** preceded by a **vowel**, add **s**.	toy**s**, birthday**s**, key**s**	
5. If a nouns ends with **y** preceded by a **consonant**, drop the **y** and add **ies**.	bunn**ies**, penn**ies**	
6. If a noun ends with **o** preceded by a **vowel**, add **s**.	cameo**s**, radio**s**	
7. If a noun ends with **o** preceded by a **consonant**, add **es**.	tomato**es**, potato**es**, hero**es**	musical terms (*pianos, sopranos, altos, concertos*...) and *zoos*
8. Invariable nouns	deer, fish, sheep, offspring, salmon	
9. Irregular nouns	man/men, woman/women, child/children, foot/feet, die/dice, mouse/mice, tooth/teeth, goose/geese, ox/oxen	

Plural Nouns
Some nouns are always plural.
Examples: clothes, sunglasses, pants, scissors, pyjamas
Zero and volcano can be written either way in the plural (zeros/zeroes, volcanos/volcanoes)

⚠ PAY ATTENTION!

NON-COUNT NOUNS
- Non-count nouns are always singular.
- They are things that cannot be counted.
- They often express qualities, substances, abstract things or collective names for count nouns like:
- **furniture** (tables, chairs, beds, etc.)
- **money** (dollars, euros, quarters, etc.)
- In English, *advice, furniture, hair, news, homework, information* and *spaghetti* are all non-count nouns and have no plural form.

Practise!

Make the nouns in bold plural.

a) *Mouse* (_____) are a problem in some **city** (_____).

b) He dropped the **dish** (_____) and the **glass** (_____) while clearing the **table** (_____).

c) Montreal's skyline is dotted with **cross** (_____) from its numerous **church** (_____).

d) Those stained-glass **window** (_____) are magnificent.

e) The **child** (_____) play in the park under the supervision of their **mother** (_____).

f) He is not a very good dancer. He has two left **foot** (_____).

Unit 1 ▪ At All Costs

Name: _____ Date: _____ Group: _____

Focus on...

Articles

Indefinite Articles	
SINGULAR	**PLURAL**
(a/an)	(–/some)

Use indefinite articles for objects that are **not specific**.

Examples: *She is riding **a** bicycle.*
(a bicycle in general)
Apples are good for you.
(apples in general)

Use the indefinite article **the first time** you speak of something:

Examples: *She found **a** wallet.*
*He is **a** busboy in a restaurant.*

Definite Articles	
SINGULAR	**PLURAL**
(the)	(the)

Use definite articles for objects that are **specific** or **unique**. It is clear which particular objects are being referred to.

Examples: *She is riding **the** bicycle I gave her yesterday.*
*May I have **the** green apple?*

Use the definite article **the second time** you speak of something:

Examples: ***The** wallet contained a lot of money.*
***The** restaurant is downtown.*

Some/Any
- Use some for an **INDEFINITE** number or quantity in an affirmative statement:
I need some help.
We want some answers.
- Use any with negative statements:
I don't have any money.
They don't want any food.

Do not use articles for:
- sports
- hobbies, activities and school subjects
- names of streets, roads, avenues...
- languages
- names of continents
- names of countries
(Exceptions: **the** United States, **the** Republic of China)

Use definite articles for:
- names of rivers, oceans and seas
- names of deserts, forests, gulfs, peninsulas and mountain ranges

Examples: ***the** Atlantic,*
***the** Rockies*

Practise!

Write the appropriate articles (a, an, the, any, some) or indicate NA (not applicable) in the spaces provided.

My Short Autobiography

My parents were both born in _____ Italy. They lived in _____ small village of Pellaro near _____ capital of _____ Calabria, _____ Reggio. It was a small village just like _____ small village you find along the coast in southern Italy. In 1951, my father immigrated to _____ Canada, or more specifically, _____ Quebec.

I was raised as _____ Quebecer. I went to _____ English school to begin with, but my parents then transferred me to _____ French school. In school, I liked _____ sports more than others. But I definitely liked _____ sports more than _____ English or _____ French. I played _____ softball and _____ hockey. I particularly liked _____ football. I did not excel in any sport in particular, but I enjoyed them all.

Today, I teach _____ English in high school and I live with my beautiful wife in _____ house by _____ Richelieu River.

4 Unit 1 ▪ At All Costs

Name: _____ Date: _____ Group: _____

Focus on...
Quantifiers with Count and Non-count Nouns

With **count nouns** only ⟶ A couple of, a few, several, many
With **non-count nouns** only ⟶ A little, much, a great deal of
With **count nouns** AND **non-count nouns** ⟶ Any, some, a lot

Practise!

From the list above, choose the appropriate quantifier to complete the following sentences.

a) I'm having _____ of trouble with this exercise.
b) How _____ rain have we had this month?
c) The weather is bad; there's not _____ hope for sunshine.
d) We were able to destroy _____ of the parasites.
e) I don't have _____ money left.

ACTIVITY 1

Put the appropriate definite article in the blanks or indicate NA (not applicable).

a) _____ Mediterranean surrounds _____ Italian peninsula.
b) _____ Scotland is a very cold country in winter.
c) _____ Parliament Building is truly an example of great architecture.
d) _____ British Columbia is Canada's most western province.
e) _____ Mackenzie River runs from south to north.

ACTIVITY 2

Write the appropriate article in the blanks (a, an, the, some, any) or indicate NA (not applicable).

An Active Life

Linda comes from _____ Vancouver. She has travelled all over _____ world. She has practised _____ different sports on almost every continent. In _____ India, she played _____ badminton, and she swam in _____ Ganges River and rode on _____ elephant. She hiked _____ Appalachian Trail in _____ United States. She participated in a triathlon in _____ Hawaii. She has travelled to _____ Republic of China, where she visited _____ Forbidden City and won _____ table tennis competition. While she was there, she also took _____ walk along _____ Great Wall of _____ China and ate _____ local delicacies. She has been to _____ France many times and has tried to take part in _____ Tour de France. In Paris, she visited _____ Louvre, where she saw _____ Leonardo's masterpiece, _____ *Mona Lisa*. She wanted to visit _____ vineyards along the way, but there wasn't _____ time left. She loves to be on _____ go, but her home and heart is in _____ Vancouver, _____ British Columbia.

Name: _____ Date: _____ Group: _____

Pronouns and Possessive Adjectives

① Did **you** watch the game last night?

② Yeah. **It** was really exciting, wasn't **it**?

Yeah, **you**'re right. But let's not forget the rest of the team. Without **them**, **he** would have looked very stupid alone on the ice.

③ The goalie was the real hero, though. Without **him**, **we** would have lost. **He** made many great saves.

Focus on...

Personal Pronouns

Pronouns are words used to replace nouns. They act like nouns. They can be either the subject or object of the verb.

	Subject	Object
Singular	I	me
	you	you
	he/she/it	him/her/it
Plural	we	us
	you	you
	they	them
What they do:	Initiate an action	Receive an action
When to use them:	To carry out the action of the verb. They usually precede the verb.	To receive the action of the verb. They follow the verb.
Where to look for them:	Just before the verb (except in questions)	After a transitive verb. After a preposition
Examples	**She** wrote an article on cheating.	They tested **him** for illegal drugs.
	We are learning about sports ethics.	He invited **you** to the beach.
	I play hockey in Victoriaville.	We saw **them** on TV.

Practise!

Replace the expressions in bold with the appropriate pronoun.

a) **John and Sam** _____ are always getting into trouble with **their teacher** _____.

b) **Martha** _____ really loves to ski. I haven't seen **that girl** _____ often without **her skis** _____.

c) **The car** _____ broke down as I was driving to work. Now **my boss** _____ is going to be upset.

d) **The girls** _____ won't talk to **John and me** _____ anymore.

e) Where is **my bicycle** _____?

6 Unit 1 ■ At All Costs   Thank you for not photocopying.   © Éditions Grand Duc

Name: _____ Date: _____ Group: _____

ACTIVITY 3

1 Replace the underlined words with the appropriate subject or object pronoun.

2 Replace the underlined pronouns with the appropriate noun or nouns.

The 1919 World Series

The word "cheating" is usually associated with doing something wrong in order to win. Many athletes have been accused of cheating when those athletes (_____) took illegal substances to boost their performance or when someone caught the same athletes (_____) doing something contrary to the rules of the sport. But during the 1919 World Series, a group of players from the Chicago White Sox cheated – not to win, but to lose. I remember my great-grandfather telling my brother and me (_____) about the 1919 World Series (_____) and how that scandal (_____) almost destroyed the great game of baseball. Among the eight players involved in the scandal was "Shoeless" Joe Jackson. Jackson (_____) was one of Chicago's best players, but like the other seven players, Jackson (_____) thought Cominsky (the White Sox owner) was exploiting the players (_____). Cominsky (_____) didn't pay his players (_____) what they were worth. For example, he promised a $10,000 bonus if Cicotte (_____) won 30 games in the season. Cicotte had almost reached his goal when Cominsky (_____) had Cicotte (_____) benched.

They (_____) were to receive $40,000 if they (_____) decided to throw the series. The signal that they had accepted the deal was the following: Cicotte would have to hit the first batter he (_____) pitched against. The first pitch was a strike. The second pitch hit him (_____) square in the back. It (_____) was on.

They (_____) lost the first game by a score of 9-1. They (_____) also lost the second but won the third. After they (_____) received $20,000, they lost the fourth and fifth games. The money was not coming in as promised, so they (_____) won the sixth and seventh games. A man was sent to speak to one of the players' wives. He (_____) told her (_____) that if he (_____) did not lose the next game, she (_____) would be in grave danger of bodily harm. They (_____) lost it (_____).

After the 1919 series was over, an article appeared in the *New York World*. It (_____) suggested that the series had been fixed. A Grand Jury was convened to investigate the allegations. This led to a trial. It (_____) lasted until 1921. At the end, the eight players left the courthouse scot-free. They (_____) were acquitted of all charges, but the presiding judge banned them (_____) from baseball for life.

© Éditions Grand Duc   Thank you for not photocopying.   Unit 1 ■ At All Costs   **7**

Name: _____ Date: _____ Group: _____

Focus on...

Possessive Adjectives, Possessive Pronouns and Reflexive Pronouns

Possessive adjectives and pronouns are used to show ownership.
Reflexive pronouns refer back to the subject.

Possessive Adjectives and Pronouns		Reflexive Pronouns
Possessive Adjectives	**Possessive Pronouns**	
my	mine	myself
your	yours	yourself
his	his	himself
her	hers	herself
its	its	itself
our	ours	ourselves
your	yours	yourselves
their	theirs	themselves

⚠️ **PAY ATTENTION!**

Be careful not to confuse **it's** (it is) and **its** (possessive adjective)!
It's raining! The dog is chasing its tail.

⚠️ **PAY ATTENTION!**

The possessive adjective always refers to the person who is the owner: Jane's book = **her** book.

	When to Use Them	Examples
Possessive Adjectives	To show ownership They agree with the "possessor," not the object.	Angela lost **his** skateboard. (John's) Angela lost **her** skateboard. (Angela's) Someone stole **our** skateboard.
Possessive Pronouns	To show ownership They replace a possessive adjective and the noun it modifies.	That skateboard is **hers**. (Angela's) That surfboard belongs to me; it is **mine**. The future is **yours**.
Reflexive Pronouns	When the subject and the object are the same **by** + reflexive pronoun = without others; without help	You should give **yourselves** a pat on the back for being such good sports. They are playing **by themselves**. He won the game all **by himself**.

Practise!

Replace the underlined phrase with the appropriate possessive pronoun.

a) We can eat all the pizza we want. It's <u>our pizza</u> (_____).

b) The key wouldn't unlock the car because it wasn't <u>my key</u> (_____).

c) I don't have any money. Do you have <u>your money</u> (_____)?

d) This house isn't <u>your house</u> (_____). It's <u>her house</u> (_____).

8 | Unit 1 ■ At All Costs

ACTIVITY 4

Replace the word "alone" with the preposition "by" and a *reflexive pronoun*.

a) She studied alone. _____

b) The two boys went to the store alone. _____

c) The dog walked home alone. _____

d) Some people like to study alone. _____

e) John and I will practice alone. _____

f) He lives alone. _____

g) Do you usually travel alone? _____

h) Susan and Henry will paint their apartment alone. _____
_____

i) I sometimes like to train alone. _____

j) Mary usually eats alone. _____

ACTIVITY 5

Highlight or circle the correct answer.

a) Our teacher does not like his students to ask him questions until they first try to figure the problem out on (their/theirs/they/there) own.

b) Jack is a very shallow person. He only likes people for (there/their/theirs/them) beauty.

c) A wolf will call (it/its/it's) pups by howling.

d) The bathroom is (her/hers) to clean, not (my/mine/me/I).

e) We never thought (our/ours/we) class would win the spelling championship.

f) My pancakes are thinner than (her/hers/she).

g) Did you lose (yours/you/your/you're) skates?

h) (It's/Its/It) my job to clean (mine/my/me/I) room every week.

i) I saw (her/hers/she) expression. It was not pretty.

j) I remember looking for (ours/our/we) telephone book.

Name: _____ Date: _____ Group: _____

Focus on...

Indefinite Pronouns

Indefinite pronouns do not specify what noun they replace.

Pronouns	Characteristics	Examples
everybody (everyone) nobody (no one) somebody (someone)	• Can be the subject or object of a sentence • Are always singular • Are used only in the affirmative	• **Everybody** I know loves to watch that athlete skate. • I saw **everyone** I know there. • **Nobody** left early. • **Somebody** has a lot of explaining to do. • I found **somebody** with a cellphone.
anybody (anyone)	• Is always singular • Is used with a negative form of the verb or for questions	• I don't know **anybody** who doesn't like to watch that athlete skate. • Does **anybody** have a cellphone I can borrow?

Practise!

1. Change the following sentences to the negative form.
2. Use the correct indefinite pronoun.

Example: He said he met someone on his trip.
He said he didn't meet anyone on his trip.

a) We knew everybody at the party.
_____

b) I believe there is someone home.
_____

c) He spoke to someone about the problem.
_____

d) I gave my book to somebody.
_____

e) There seems to be someone with her.
_____

f) He told everyone about the plans.
_____

g) They left someone behind.
_____

Name: _____ Date: _____ Group: _____

ACTIVITY 6

Write the appropriate personal, possessive or reflexive pronoun in the following sentences.

A Golfing Vacation

Jack and I decided to go on a golf trip together. Since we wanted to save a bit of money, we made the preparations for the trip _____. Jack bought a new set of clubs. I told _____ that he did not have to buy any; _____ could borrow _____. _____ thanked _____ and told _____ his girlfriend had already offered _____. Jokingly, _____ asked _____ if _____ had offered her pink golf bag, also. _____ said _____ had, but _____ thought it best to refuse. _____ agreed with _____ and continued packing my own stuff.

Jack and _____ finally arrived at the airport. _____ were about three hours early, so _____ decided to relax and enjoy a cup of coffee. One hour later, _____ checked my ticket, so Jack checked _____. That's when _____ realized that _____ was the wrong day. Our flight was leaving tomorrow. Our bags had left an hour ago.

ACTIVITY 7

Write the appropriate possessive adjective or pronoun in the blanks.

A Golfing Vacation (Part Two)

We weren't going to miss out on _____ well-deserved holiday. Not if I could help it! I talked to the person in charge (I added a few tears and heavy sighs, like _____ sister used to do when she wanted to soften _____ father's heart). After hearing _____ story, the airline agreed to change _____ tickets. And off we were. Or so I thought. But Jack is special. He had brought _____ golf clubs, but had forgotten _____ luggage at home. We got in touch with _____ sister who was about to leave for South America. She brought _____ things over right away.

When we arrived at _____ hotel that evening and he opened _____ luggage to take out _____ pyjamas for the night, we realized that _____ sister Rosemary had made a mistake. The luggage was _____. Now he was stuck with women's clothing and Rosemary was on _____ way to South America with her brother's clothes. So we had to rush to buy new clothes, a comb and toothbrush for my good friend Jack. It's always an adventure travelling with him!

Unit 1 ■ At All Costs

ACTIVITY 8

Rewrite these sentences and replace the words in bold with the appropriate possessive pronouns.

Example: This room is **my** room.
This room is mine.

a) This tennis racquet is **your tennis racquet**.
___

b) That pair of skis is **her pair of skis**.
___

c) These roller blades are **their roller blades**.
___

d) This helmet is **Joe's helmet**.
___

e) That trophy is **Mr. and Mrs. Tremblay's trophy**.
___

f) The yellow golf cart is **Joan's golf cart**.
___

g) The green race car is **Francine's car**.
___

h) This radio is **my radio**.
___

i) The papers on the desk are **our papers**.
___

j) Timothy is **John's sled dog**.
___

k) The red bicycle is **Joanna's bicycle**.
___

l) These golf clubs are **their golf clubs**.
___

n) That tennis court is **Mr. and Mrs. Tremblay's tennis court**.
___

Unit 1 ■ At All Costs

Name: _____ Date: _____ Group: _____

Focus on...

Demonstrative Pronouns

Demonstrative pronouns are used to designate a **person**, **place** or **thing** that **must be pointed to**. There are four demonstrative pronouns: *this*, *that*, *these* and *those*.

	When the object is <u>near</u> the speaker	When the object is <u>at a distance</u> from the speaker	Examples
Singular	this	that	**This** is my tennis racket. **That** is her kayak.
Plural	these	those	**These** are his skis. **Those** are her skates.

ACTIVITY 9

❶ Look at the pictures. Anna and her husband are talking about some persons, places or things that are near or at a distance from them.

❷ Complete their sentences using the appropriate demonstrative pronoun.

_____ chairs are reserved.

_____ man comes from Peru.

Anna and her husband

_____ window is open.

_____ dictionary is mine.

_____ radio is very loud.

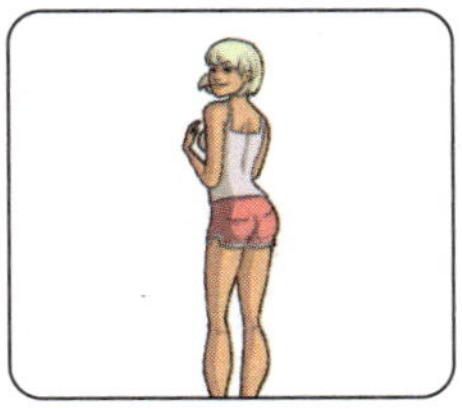

_____ girl is beautiful.

_____ guitar is very well tuned.

_____ magazines are very old.

Unit 1 ■ At All Costs   13

Name: _____ Date: _____ Group: _____

Focus on...

There Is/There Are...

There is/There are is a common structure used to indicate that something is present.

Use **there is** with **singular** nouns and **there are** with **plural** nouns.

	There Is	There Are
	With Singular Nouns	With Plural Nouns
Affirmative Form	*There is* an arena on Main Street. *There's* an arena on Main Street.	*There are* many arenas in Quebec.
Negative Form	*There is no* ice time available. *There's no* ice time available. *There isn't any* ice time available.	*There are no* tickets left. *There are zero* tickets left. *There aren't any* tickets left.

Practise!

1. Write five sentences describing your street, your hometown or your city.

2. Each sentence must contain the expression THERE IS, THERE'S, THERE ARE, THERE ISN'T or THERE AREN'T.

Example: In my town, **there is** an arena by the school.
There are three soccer fields.

a) _____

b) _____

c) _____

d) _____

e) _____

Name: _____ Date: _____ Group: _____

ACTIVITY 10

❶ Look at the following picture.

❷ Describe 10 things you see using *There is* or *There are* at the beginning of each sentence.

a) _____

b) _____

c) _____

d) _____

e) _____

f) _____

g) _____

h) _____

i) _____

j) _____

k) _____

© Éditions Grand Duc   Thank you for not photocopying.   Unit 1 ■ At All Costs

Simple Verb Tenses

① *I usually **jog** in the morning, but today I **don't** really **feel** like it.*

② *What **seems** to be the problem?*

③ *I **don't know**. I just **feel** like going back to bed. I **wonder** what is wrong with me.*

④ *Maybe the all-night party **has** something to do with it.*

⑤ *Do you think so?*

Focus on...

The Simple Present

The **simple present tense** is used:

- to describe habitual or usual activities.
  Example: *I **get up** at six every morning. I **jog** 5 kilometres every day.*

- to talk about facts.
  Example: *Hockey **is** Canada's national sport. Madrid **has** many bullfight arenas. He **lives** in Toronto now.*

- to express likes and dislikes.
  Example: *He **prefers** golf to bicycling.*

How to form it:

The **third person** singular always ends in "**s**."

Example: *He **works** very hard to correct his technique.*

Negative form:

For the negative form, use **doesn't/don't + the base form of the verb.**

Examples: *I **don't play** very well. He **doesn't like** to lose. We **don't understand** the rules of the game.*

Keywords
- usually
- often
- normally
- in general
- every morning
- in the afternoon
- before going to bed
- on Sundays (Mondays, Fridays, etc.)

Practise!

Write the verbs in parentheses in the simple present tense.

An Ideal Job

John (to be) _____ a fervent Canadiens hockey fan. He (to think) _____ he (to have) _____ the best job in the whole world. He (to work) _____ in a factory that (to make) _____ hockey sticks for professional hockey teams. The sticks his factory (to produce) _____ end up in the hands of some of the world's best players. The factory (to receive) _____ regular visits from some of the game's greatest. When this (to happen) _____, John usually (to take) _____ a few minutes from his job to talk with the players. He also (to pose) _____ for a picture that will end up in his extensive collection. Naturally, he (to ask) _____ the guys to autograph it, making it much more valuable. No, John (to have, neg.) _____ a boring job.

Name: _____ Date: _____ Group: _____

Focus on...

Questions

For the **interrogative form** in the present tense, use the auxiliary **do/does**.

Yes/No Questions

Auxiliary	Subject	Verb (Base Form)	Object
Do	you	like	hockey?
Does	he	play	the guitar?
Do	they	read	the daily paper?

Information Questions

Question Word	Auxiliary	Subject	Verb (Base Form)	Object
Where	does	he	play	hockey?
How	do	they	come	to school?
How often	do	you	read	the newspaper?

Question Tags

Question tags are a form of Yes/No question. They are used in these circumstances:

- Question tags are used in a conversation to solicit a reaction from the person you are talking to.
- Most often, but not always, this reaction will be in the affirmative form.
- Question tags are usually used in spoken conversation and very rarely in texts.
- Contractions are always used with question tags.

Use the same auxiliary for the statement and the tag.
*For a tag in the **simple present**, use **doesn't** or **don't**.*

Question Tags

Affirmative Statement → Negative Tag	Negative Statement → Affirmative Tag
This is exciting, isn't it?	He's not from here, is he?
I can come, can't I?	You wouldn't travel alone to Asia, would you?
She plays hockey, doesn't she?	You don't play football, do you?

Practise!

Write the verbs in parentheses in the present tense.

At School

We (to come) _____ to class every day. We normally (to sit, neg.) _____ at the same desk. Sometimes the teacher (to move) _____ us around. Usually, we (to work) _____ in groups, but I (to prefer) _____ to work alone. My friend Henry (to like) _____ to work in groups. He (to perform) _____ better in a group. His sister Sally (to be) _____ like me. She (to work, neg.) _____ well in a group. I usually (to come) _____ to school by bus. Sometimes Henry and I (to walk) _____ to school.

Unit 1 ■ At All Costs

Name: _____ Date: _____ Group: _____

ACTIVITY 11

Write the following sentences in the interrogative form as indicated:
Y/N = Yes/No question, Info = information question, TAG = question tag.

> Examples: Athletes eat a lot of pasta. (Y/N) *Do athletes eat a lot of pasta?*
> Koalas live in Australia (Info) *Where do koalas live?*
> The children eat breakfast at seven-thirty. (TAG)
> *The children eat breakfast at seven-thirty, don't they?*

a) The Richelieu River is the biggest river in Quebec. (Y/N)
_____

b) Every spring there is a festival that takes place in the Chambly Rapids. (Info)
_____

c) People enjoy the thrill of swimming the rapids. (TAG)
_____

d) The Chambly Rapids are 2.5 kilometres long. (Info)
_____

e) The activity is dangerous if you don't swim well. (Y/N)
_____

f) People don't try it if they are afraid. (TAG)
_____
_____

g) John and Arthur participate in the swim every year. (Y/N)
_____
_____

h) They just love the adrenalin rush it produces. (TAG)
_____
_____

i) They are both excellent swimmers. (Y/N)
_____
_____

j) Arthur's girlfriend usually accompanies him on this adventure. (Info)
_____

Name: _____ Date: _____ Group: _____

ACTIVITY 12

① Use the verbs in the Word Bank to complete the text. A verb may be used more than once.
② Write the verbs in the simple present tense.

Word Bank						
• attend	• be	• break	• clothe	• cost	• do	• earn
• feed	• get	• give	• know	• lead	• live	• make
• meet	• participate	• pick	• prepare	• put	• rent	• respect
• share	• stay		• want	• work		

A Letter from Mendoza

I usually _____ in many soccer tournaments. During these tournaments, I _____ very interesting people. Once I visited a vineyard in the region of Mendoza. There I worked for a few days with a man named Santiago. When I left, I asked him to write a small text presenting himself to my students. Here it _____:

Hello, my name _____ Santiago. I _____ in a small village in Argentina. My major occupation _____ harvesting grapes to make wine. I _____ every day from seven in the morning to six in the evening. Since the sun _____ very hot around noon, we _____ for lunch between twelve and two o'clock.

We _____ the house we _____ in from the vineyard's owner. My wife, Alejandra, my daughter, Mili (which _____ short for Milagro meaning miracle), my father, Martin, my mother, Julia, and my sister, Marisol, _____ the house. My father also picks grapes with me. The women stay home and _____ the food for all the men. My sister _____ what you would call high school. She _____ in her last year there. She _____ to become an engineer, but that _____ a lot of money. So, she also _____ in the fields, and the money she _____, she _____ aside to pay for her studies.

It _____ a hard life we _____, but it _____ satisfying. We _____ with our hands and we _____ that our work _____ other people around the world happy. Our wine is the best in the region and that _____ because the grapes _____ picked with love and attention. We _____ the land we _____ on because it _____ us, it _____ us and it _____ us life.

I hope you will come and visit my family one day.

Unit 1 ■ At All Costs   19

Name: _____ Date: _____ Group: _____

① What **did** you do last week?

② I **participated** in a soccer tournament in South America.

③ Really! **Did** you **visit** a few countries?

④ I **visited** Peru, Argentina and Brazil.

⑤ All in one week?

⑥ Yeah!

⑦ When **did** you **play** soccer?

Focus on...

The Simple Past

The **simple past tense** is used to describe an action that took place and was finished sometime in the past.

How to form it:

To form the past tense, add **-ed**, **-id** or **-ied** to the base form of the regular verbs.

Examples: He **trained** very hard all year for this competition.
George **retired** from his position as coach.
She **carried** her heavy bag to the gym.

> ⚠️ **PAY ATTENTION!**
>
> **Irregular verbs:**
>
> Irregular verbs must be memorized.
>
> Examples: I **lost** the first game of the season.
> My brother **bought** a new golf bag.

Keywords
- yesterday
- last night
- last week
- the other day
- long ago...

Negative form:

For the negative form, use **didn't + base form of the verb.**

Examples: We **didn't see** the final game of the Stanley Cup playoffs.
She **didn't have** time to finish.

Interrogative form:

For the **interrogative form**, use the auxiliary **did**.

– Yes/No questions: auxiliary + subject + base form of the verb

Example: **Did** she **participate** in last year's marathon?

– Information questions: question word + auxiliary + subject + base form of the verb

Example: **Where did** they **play** their last round of golf?

– Question tags: Use **didn't** in the simple past.

Example: Mario cheated on that last hole, **didn't** he?

20   Unit 1 ■ At All Costs   Thank you for not photocopying.   © Éditions Grand Duc

Name: _____ Date: _____ Group: _____

ACTIVITY 13

1. **Write the verb in parentheses in the simple past tense.**
2. **Write the sentences in the interrogative form as indicated:**
   Y/N = Yes/No question, Info = information question and TAG = question tag.

   a) The movie (to begin) _____ at ten o'clock. (Info)
   _____

   b) They (to eat) _____ lunch at a fancy restaurant. (Y/N)
   _____

   c) You (to walk) _____ to school with Jean. (TAG)
   _____

   d) He (to pay) _____ for lunch with a check. (Info)
   _____

   e) They (to go) _____ home after school. (TAG)
   _____

   f) Sam (to live) _____ there for five years. (Y/N)
   _____

   g) Helen (to explain) _____ the problem in Spanish. (Info)
   _____

   h) The lesson (to last) _____ two hours. (Info)
   _____

   i) You (to hear) _____ the telephone last night. (TAG)
   _____

   j) She (to put) _____ on her grey coat. (TAG)
   _____

   k) The tournament (to start) _____ last weekend. (Info)
   _____

   l) Last year's winner (to walk) _____ away with
   $100,000. (Y/N)
   _____

   m) They (to celebrate) _____ the victory very noisily. (TAG)
   _____

© Éditions Grand Duc — Thank you for not photocopying. — Unit 1 ▪ At All Costs — 21

ACTIVITY 14

Write the verbs in parentheses in the past tense.

Ancient Sports

This morning, class (to begin) _____ at nine o'clock. During class, we (to read) _____ about sports (to play) _____ hundreds or even thousands of years ago. Some (to be) _____ quite different than the sports we watch or practise today, others (to be) _____ almost the same.

The Mayan (to play) _____ a ball game using a rubber ball about 50 centimetres in diameter. The object of the game (to be) _____ to pass the rubber ball through a hoop (to situate) _____ high on one of the walls of the court. The rules (to seem) _____ simple enough. The players could not touch the ball with their hands, like today's soccer. They (to pass) _____ the ball continuously. It (to be) _____ extremely difficult to score and the game usually (to end) _____ when one of two things (to happen) _____: either a team (to score) _____ or the ball (to hit) _____ the ground. Winners (to be) _____ considered heroes, but unfortunately losers (to be) _____ not. The captain of the losing team (to be) _____ sacrificed to the gods.

We also (to learn) _____ that sports we (to think) _____ to be very modern are actually very old. Take soccer for example: an ancient game (to play) _____ in China (to call) _____ Tsu-Chu (to resemble) _____ soccer very much. The object of the game (to be) _____ to kick a ball through an opening in a small net. The Japanese (to have) _____ a game they (to name) _____ Kemari that (to look) _____ like our modern game of Aki. It was played with a 24 centimetre deerskin ball (to fill) _____ with sawdust. The game (to consist) _____ in keeping the ball from touching the floor while juggling it with their feet. The players (to have) _____ to keep the ball airborne by passing it from one to another. They (to play) _____ the game on a rectangular playing field (to call) _____ kikutsubo. The game is still around today.

Many sports we practise today were played in ancient Egypt. Naturally, swimming (to be) _____ a popular sport among the Egyptians, the Nile being one great big pool in which they (to swim) _____. They (to hold) _____ swimming competitions of every sort. Amazingly, a variation of hockey (to seems) _____ to have been played in Ancient Egypt. Drawings in tombs show players holding long curved sticks that resemble hockey sticks. The ball was made of papyrus fibres and was painted with two or more colours. Five thousand year-old drawings show people (to engage) _____ in what seems to be a game of handball. The ball, (to make) _____ of leather and (to stuff) _____ with various materials, (to be) _____ lightweight and probably (to use) _____ only once.

So, today we (to learn) _____ that many sports that resemble those we play today (to be) _____ around a long time ago.

Name: _____ Date: _____ Group: _____

ACTIVITY 15

1 Look at the pictures below and write a question asking about what they did yesterday or sometime in the past. Include a tense marker or keyword, such as yesterday, last night, etc.

2 Answer the question.

_____
_____

_____
_____

_____
_____

_____
_____

_____
_____

_____
_____

Unit 1 ■ At All Costs

Name: _____ Date: _____ Group: _____

① *Where **will** you **go** next time?*

② *I'm **going to go** to Hawaii.*

③ *What **will** you **do** there?*

④ *I'll **compete** in the Ironman competition.*

Focus on...

The Simple Future

The **simple future tense** is used to express a future action.

How to form it:

a) Use: **will + base form of the verb**

   Examples: He **will play** soccer tonight, but he **won't be** goalie. (will not be)
   We **will be** there, but we **won't stay** too late.
   After the Olympics, he **will be** famous all over the country.

b) You can also use: **to be going to + base form of the verb**

   Examples: He **is going to play** soccer tonight, but he **isn't going to be** goalie.
   We**'re going to be** there, but we **aren't going to stay** too late.
   After the Olympics, he **is going to be** famous all over the country.

Negative form:

a) Use: **will not (won't) + base form of the verb**

   Example: They **will not make (won't make)** the team with that attitude.

b) You can also use: **to be + not + going to + verb**

   Examples: They **are not going to make** the team with that attitude.
   They **aren't going to make** the team with that attitude.

Keywords
- soon
- in five minutes
- later
- next month
- tomorrow
- in three days
- when I'm old
- in a little while
- after that
- from now on
- in the future
- any second now
- next
- shortly...

Interrogative form:

– Yes/No questions:
will + subject + verb
OR to be + subject + going to + verb

   Examples: a) **Will** you **participate** in the tournament?
   b) **Are** you **going to participate** in the tournament?

– Question tags:

Use **will/won't** or **to be** in the present tense.

   Examples: a) He will go to the arena, **won't** he?
   He won't go to the arena, **will** he?
   b) He's going to buy new skates, **isn't** he?
   He isn't going to buy them, **is** he?

– Information questions:

question word + will + subject + verb OR question word + to be going to + verb

   Examples: a) Where **will** you **be** tomorrow?
   b) What **are** you **going to do** later?

Practise!

Read the sentences. Change WILL for TO BE GOING TO.

Examples: They *will visit* us next year.
They *are going to visit us next year.*

a) My cousin will travel to British Columbia soon.
_____

b) Frank will participate in the Winter Olympics.
_____

c) My brother will win a medal in the downhill competition.
_____

d) I will take the train to Whistler.
_____

e) We will be there to cheer him on to victory.
_____

ACTIVITY 16

Write the following sentences in the negative form, then complete the sentence with an affirmative statement.

Examples: We are going to visit John next week.
We are not going to visit John next week; we are going to see him in two weeks.

a) We are going to stay with him for a week.
_____

b) Sarah is going to join us there.
_____

c) She will arrive one week later.
_____

d) Sarah and her friends are going to leave before us.
_____

e) They will travel by plane to Paris.
_____

f) They will meet many important people there.
_____

g) I am going to spend all my summer on the road.
_____

Name: _____ Date: _____ Group: _____

ACTIVITY 17

Write the following sentences in the interrogative form as indicated:
Y/N = Yes/No question, Info = information question and TAG = question tag.

a) He will be home for Christmas. (TAG)
_____

b) There will be snow during the month of December. (Info)
_____

c) They are going to go to bed early tonight. (TAG)
_____

d) The game is going to start at nine o'clock. (Info)
_____

e) Everyone will arrive at seven. (Y/N)
_____

f) Martha is not going to stay home today. (TAG)
_____

g) I'm going to eat at my favourite restaurant after the game tomorrow. (Y/N)
_____

h) It is going to rain later on today. (TAG)
_____

i) The sun is going to shine tomorrow. (Y/N)
_____

j) Bob and Joe are going to eat at a restaurant tonight. (Info)
_____

k) I am going to watch the football game Sunday. (Info)
_____

l) The game will start later than expected. (Y/N)
_____

m) They are going to leave for Europe tomorrow. (TAG)
_____

n) Donald will buy tickets for the finals. (Y/N)
_____

o) George is going to start a new team. (Y/N)
_____

Unit 1 ■ At All Costs

ACTIVITY 18

YOUR FUTURE

1. Write 10 sentences describing how you see your future.
2. Write what you will do and won't do.
3. Use WILL for five sentences.
4. Use GOING TO for the five other sentences.
5. You may also use the interrogative form!

a) _____

b) _____

c) _____

d) _____

e) _____

f) _____

g) _____

h) _____

i) _____

j) _____

ACTIVITY 19 **Above and Beyond**

Some people say that history has a way of repeating itself.

1 Make 10 predictions about the future based on the past.

2 Highlight the verbs in the *past tense* and underline the verbs in the *future tense*.

Examples: There **were** two great wars in the 20th century; humanity **did not learn** from the first and **committed** the same mistake again.
I predict that man will commit that same error once again in the next 50 years.

Or on a happier note:

Examples: Through his perseverance, man **struggled** to find cures for many deadly diseases.
I predict that within 20 years we will find a cure for AIDS.

a) _____

b) _____

c) _____

d) _____

e) _____

f) _____

g) _____

h) _____

i) _____

j) _____

28 Unit 1 ■ At All Costs

Name: _____ Date: _____ Group: _____

UNIT 1 — Wrap-up

ACTIVITY A

Fill in the blanks with one of the following: THERE IS/THERE ARE, THIS, THAT, THESE, THOSE, POSSESSIVE ADJECTIVES, POSSESSIVE PRONOUNS, PERSONAL PRONOUNS or REFLEXIVE PRONOUNS.

a) _____ many people who practise sports in the world today.

b) _____ also many countries where sport is a major concern of the government.

c) _____ countries have a large budget dedicated to physical education.

d) The governments of _____ countries do what is necessary to help _____ athletes.

e) _____ is not very easy to look at all _____ athletes and not realize that we can do something like that for our children, too.

f) Although _____ many organizations out there trying to help, _____ is not enough.

g) _____ sit comfortably in _____ living room watching television and thinking to _____ how easy _____ all looks.

h) But _____ know _____ is not that easy.

i) _____ need to work at _____. _____ things _____ simply must do.

j) _____ have to lift _____ off _____ chair and get busy.

k) _____ activities that don't require a lot of effort. Walking is one of them.

l) _____ don't have to run a marathon. All _____ have to do is leave the car at home every once in a while.

m) _____ friends have all started doing that. _____ are now in greater shape than _____ have ever been.

n) _____ guys used to be the biggest couch potatoes _____ had ever seen. Now _____ day starts off with a brisk walk and _____ evening ends with a casual stroll.

o) _____ governments may want to help by investing money in sports programs, but _____ all boils down to what do _____ want to do to help _____.

p) To stay active or not to stay active; _____ is the question!

© Éditions Grand Duc — Thank you for not photocopying. — Unit 1 ■ At All Costs — 29

Name: _____ Date: _____ Group: _____

ACTIVITY B

Complete the crossword puzzle and find the mystery message.

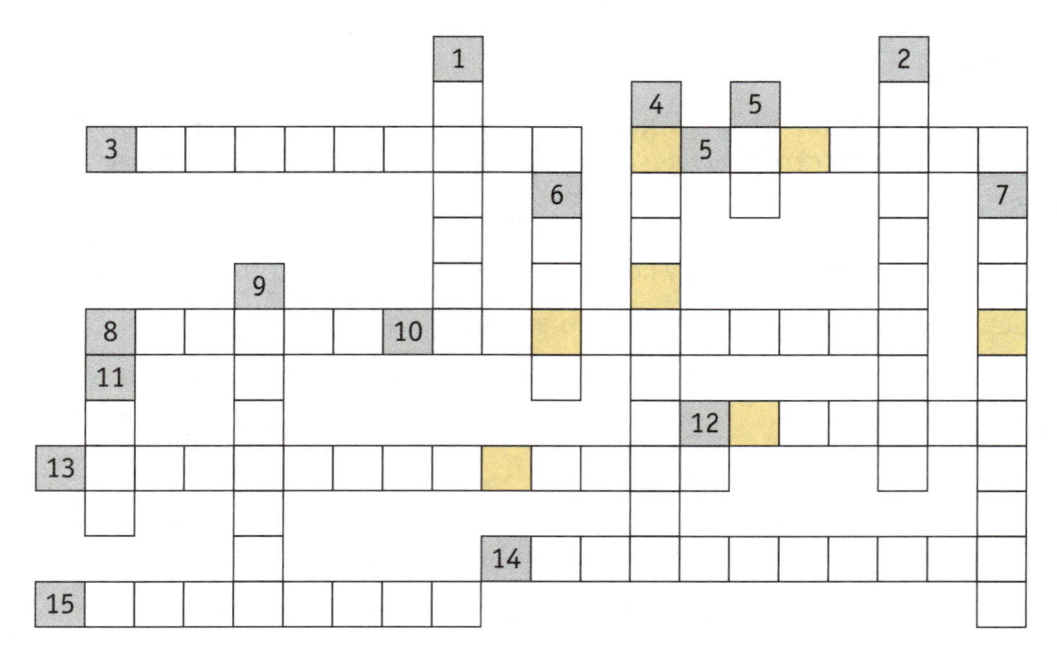

A pronoun is a noun that has lost its _ _ _ _ _ _ _ status.

ACROSS

3. An indefinite pronoun used only in the affirmative and, although singular, has a plural meaning.
5. Where a personal pronoun subject is placed with regard to the verb.
8. Number of reflexive pronouns that express the plural.
10. Plural of yourself.
12. An indefinite pronoun always used with a negative form of the verb.
13. Sentence form where the personal pronoun subject is **not** placed before the auxiliary.
14. A type of pronoun that shows ownership.
15. An indefinite pronoun that is always singular.

DOWN

1. Add the correct pronoun: Everybody left the party very late; _____ left early.
2. What a possessive adjective agrees with.
4. When two or more people do something without any help, they do it by _____.
5. A word that is placed before a reflexive pronoun to show that it was done without help.
6. Possessive adjective, second person.
7. Jack, Sonia, Oliver, Jim and I did it by _____.
9. Personal pronouns, object form _____ the action of the verb.
11. A possessive adjective that is identical to the possessive pronoun.

30 Unit 1 • At All Costs   Thank you for not photocopying.   © Éditions Grand Duc

ACTIVITY C

Fill in the blanks with the correct form of the verbs in parentheses.

a) Last night, I (to have) _____ the weirdest dream. I (to dream) _____ that I (to be) _____ in a deep green forest. There I (to meet) _____ an old man who (to say) _____ to me, "Please, sit and talk for a while." So I (to sit) _____ and we (to start) _____ to talk. Suddenly, he (to open) _____ his mouth and (to scream) _____ very loudly. That (to be) _____ when my alarm (to go) _____ off.

b) There (to be) _____ nights when I (to dream) _____ about more pleasant things than an old man screaming. I sometimes (to participate) _____ in the Olympics. I (to run) _____ the 100 metres and as I (to be) _____ about to cross the finish line, the ground under my feet (to turn) _____ to quicksand and I (to sink) _____. So there I (to stand) _____, my feet in quicksand as I (to watch) _____ the other competitors (to cross) _____ the finish line ahead of me.

c) Every night, it (to be) _____ the same thing. I (to have) _____ these weird dreams and I (know, neg.) _____ what they mean. When I (to wake) _____ up in the morning, I (to feel) _____ strange. My friend always (to try) _____ to give me advice, but I (to think) _____ that he just (to want) _____ to seem important.

d) I (to wonder) _____ if I (to have) _____ these dreams forever. I (to think) _____ I (to see) _____ a psychiatrist; I (to be) _____ sure he (to help) _____ me. I (to think) _____ I (to need) _____ help. My dreams (to be) _____ stranger and stranger. Now, not just old people, but animals too, (to talk) _____. They (to say) _____ the most bizarre things: things like "How (to be) _____ you today?" or "How (to be, you) _____ tomorrow?" According to them, I (to know) _____ how I (to feel) _____ tomorrow. When I (to ask) _____ them what the secret (to be) _____, I usually (to wake) _____. Yesterday, I almost (to get) _____ the answer, but my mother (to call) _____ me because I (to be) _____ late for school. Maybe tonight I (to find out) _____ what the secret (to be) _____.

Unit 1 ■ At All Costs

Name: _____ Date: _____ Group: _____

ACTIVITY D

Write the following sentences in the interrogative form and answer in the negative contracted form. *You may use "some" and "any" where appropriate.*

Examples: There are many different nationalities in the city.
INT: *Are there many different nationalities in the city?*
NEG: *There aren't many different nationalities in the city.*

a) There is a grocery store on the corner.
_____
_____

b) There are many places where we can buy gasoline in town.
_____
_____

c) There are houses for sale on this street.
_____
_____

d) There are many good restaurants in this town.
_____
_____

e) There are some arenas in our city.
_____
_____

f) There is a hockey game every week.
_____
_____

g) There are basketball and tennis courts in our city.
_____
_____

h) There is a golf club in the region.
_____
_____

i) There is a new gym on Main Street.
_____
_____

32   Unit 1 ■ At All Costs   Thank you for not photocopying.   © Éditions Grand Duc

Name: _____ Date: _____ Group: _____

ACTIVITY E

Complete the crossword puzzle and find the mystery message.

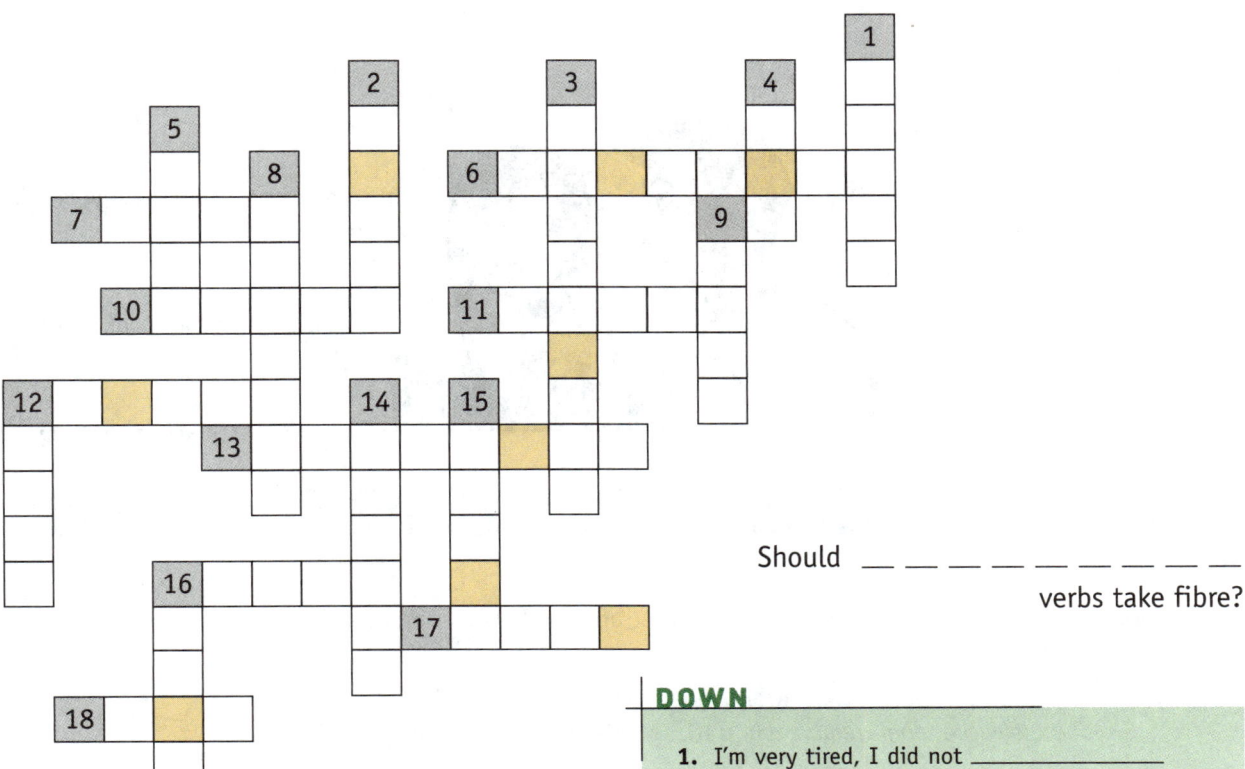

Should _ _ _ _ _ _ _ _ _
verbs take fibre?

DOWN

1. I'm very tired, I did not _____ at all last night.
2. When your car won't stop, it's probably because your brakes _____.
3. A past tense marker which is also the title of a Beatles song.
4. The auxiliary used to form the interrogative in the past tense.
5. An auxiliary used to form the simple present negative.
8. I _____ about what you said and the answer is yes.
9. I _____ all the answers in yesterday's test.
12. Past tense of what happened when you cut yourself.
14. Last month, my girlfriend _____ a new car.
15. _____ and through are homonyms.
16. Red and _____ are also homonyms.

ACROSS

6. If the statement is affirmative, the tag ending is _____.
7. It _____ her a pretty penny.
10. The Prime Minister finally _____ on that subject.
11. To finish something, you must first _____.
12. The present tense of brought is _____.
13. A kind of activity described by the simple present tense.
16. The doorbell _____.
17. A modal used to indicate the future.
18. A type of question added on to an affirmative or negative statement.

© Éditions Grand Duc   Thank you for not photocopying.   Unit 1 ■ At All Costs   **33**

Name: _____ Date: _____ Group: _____

UNIT 2 Tuning In !

Adverbs

① The place is **so** noisy, I can hardly hear the music.

② What?

③ I said it is **too** noisy in here.

④ I'm sorry, I can **barely** hear you. It's **really** noisy.

⑤ I said, it's **incredibly** loud.

⑥ Yeah, I like it too. Cool, huh!

> **Focus on...**
>
> ### Adverbs
>
> An **adverb** modifies a verb, an adjective or another adverb. It adds description and detail to your writing and speaking.
>
> Examples: She plays the violin **remarkably**. (modifies the verb *plays*)
> She plays the violin remarkably **well**. (modifies the adverb *well*)
>
> There are four basic categories of adverbs:
> 1. adverbs of **frequency**
> 2. adverbs of **time**
> 3. adverbs of **manner**
> 4. adverbs of **intensity and degree**
>
> Some adverbs are spelled the same way as the adjectives.
> *Examples:* fast, hard, far, first, early
> *Exceptions:* good – well, bad – worse

Practise!

Highlight the adverb and underline the word it modifies in the following sentences.

a) She plays the piano beautifully.

b) She usually practises in the afternoon.

c) She doesn't live very far from the conservatory.

d) The band is pretty good, isn't it?

e) They play their music too loudly.

f) He studied the violin for almost two whole years.

Focus on...

Adverbs of Frequency

Adverbs of frequency are used to indicate the **regularity of actions**.

They are placed before the verb, unless the verb is *to be*. When the verb includes an auxiliary, the adverb of frequency is placed between the auxiliary and the verb.

Examples: He **occasionally** arrives late for rehearsal.
He is **always** playing the same piece.
You are **seldom** late.

| never / never ever | almost never | seldom / rarely / hardly ever | occasionally | sometimes | frequently / often | usually / generally / normally | always |

Practise!

Rewrite the following sentences and put the adverbs of frequency in the right place.

a) I wanted to hear that orchestra play. (always)
_____

b) A symphony orchestra travels a lot. (usually)
_____

c) The Montreal Symphony Orchestra plays popular music. (sometimes)
_____

d) They play in major cities around the world. (often)
_____

e) Members of the Montreal Symphony Orchestra are virtuosos. (generally)
_____

f) They practise their repertoire. (frequently)
_____

g) Even if they are excellent musicians, they skip rehearsals. (never)
_____

h) During a performance, they make mistakes. (rarely)
_____

Name: _____ Date: _____ Group: _____

Focus on...

Adverbs of Time

Adverbs of time are used to indicate **when actions take place**.

They refer to the past, the present or future.

Adverbs of time frequently employ expressions with two or more words.

PAST	PRESENT	FUTURE
Examples: • **Yesterday**, I went shopping with my friends. • That CD came out **last year**. • When I arrived, she was **already** there. • We left **on Sunday**.	*Examples:* • They are going to the mall **this afternoon**. • There is a concert **tonight**. • I am **finally** done practicing! • He's **still** in the car sleeping.	*Examples:* • He will arrive **eventually**. • She's babysitting **tomorrow night**. • She will be back **soon**. • **On Saturday**, we're having a jam session.

Common Adverbs of Time

- Once upon a time, once
- yesterday
- tonight, today, tomorrow
- next week, last month
- on Friday, Saturday
- before, after
- later on
- in the future
- someday, one day
- ever, now, then, yet

Yet is used in interrogative and negative sentences.

Examples:
- Has he finished his sonata **yet**?
- No, he hasn't finished his sonata **yet**.

Still is used in positive and interrogative sentences and is placed after the auxiliary and before the main verb.

Examples:
- I am **still** waiting for their latest CD.
- Do you **still** play the piano?

Practise!

Choose the adverbs from the Word Bank to complete the text.

Stage Band

The stage band practice _____ is very important because the annual stage band competition will take place _____. Every member of the band wants to perform well. Some members will _____ go on to study music at a higher level. They might get hired _____ by a prestigious organization such as the Montreal Symphony Orchestra. Others will simply play their instruments because they enjoy it. _____, they will probably be the type of person who, _____ and _____, relaxes and gets rid of the daily tension by playing a bit of music for a couple of hours.

Word Bank
- eventually
- in the future
- next week
- now
- someday
- then
- this evening

36 Unit 2 ■ Tuning In!   Thank you for not photocopying.   © Éditions Grand Duc

Name: _____ Date: _____ Group: _____

Focus on...

Adverbs of Manner

Adverbs of manner are used to indicate **how actions are done**.

Very often they end in **ly**.

They are usually placed after the main verb or after the object. They should never be placed between the verb and the object.

Example: He played the piano **beautifully**.

ACTIVITY 1

Choose the adverbs from the Word Bank to complete the following sentences.

Word Bank

- briskly
- comfortably
- energetically
- enthusiastically
- graciously
- immediately
- magnificently
- newly
- noisily
- patiently
- quickly
- quietly
- solemnly
- suddenly
- thoroughly

a) The audience talked _____ as the orchestra warmed up.

b) Everyone was seated _____ in the _____ renovated concert hall.

c) They were waiting _____ for the orchestra to begin.

d) The soloists _____ entered the scene.

e) The hall _____ became quiet once the conductor appeared.

f) The maestro _____ raised his baton for the opening piece.

g) The audience _____ enjoyed the program and applauded _____.

h) The conductor _____ offered an encore, which was also performed _____.

i) The audience once again responded _____.

j) After the applause died down, the musicians _____ and _____ left the stage.

Unit 2 ■ Tuning In!

Name: _____ Date: _____ Group: _____

Focus on...

Adverbs of Intensity and Degree

Adverbs of Intensity and Degree show extent.

- **Adverbs of intensity** modify adjectives or other adverbs. They go **before** the adjectives or adverb they modify.

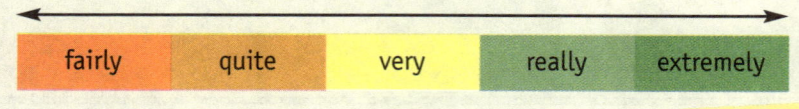

fairly	quite	very	really	extremely

Examples: Beethoven's *Ninth Symphony* is **extremely** beautiful.
He plays the piano **very** well.

- **Adverbs of degree** modify verbs. They go **after** the verb.

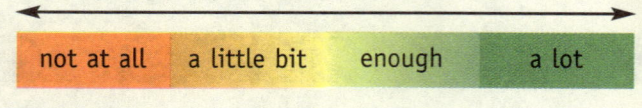

not at all	a little bit	enough	a lot

More Adverbs of Intensity and Degree
almost, nearly, quite, just, too, hardly, scarcely, completely, very, rather, fairly, too, only, so, absolutely, awfully, considerably, deeply, drastically, especially, immensely, intensely, practically, profoundly, rather, somewhat, terribly, totally, tremendously, truly, unbelievably, uncontrollably...

Examples: He practised **a lot**.
We tried **a little bit**.

When used as an adverb, the word **enough** is always placed after the word it modifies.

Example: He practised **enough** for one day.

Practise!

Choose the adverbs from the Word Bank to complete the following sentences.

Word Bank

- absolutely
- almost
- considerably
- practically
- profoundly
- somewhat
- unbelievably
- very

a) They _____ love classical music and possess _____ every record ever produced.

b) They worked _____ hard on their latest CD.

c) I was _____ moved by Schubert's *Ave Maria* played by that rock band.

d) That guitarist is _____ talented for such a _____ young age.

e) He _____ invented that _____ bizarre style of guitar playing.

Unit 2 ■ Tuning In!

Name: _____ Date: _____ Group: _____

ACTIVITY 2 — Above and Beyond

Underline the adverbs of time in the following text.

Dreams Then... and Now

My story could start with "Once upon a time..." but it won't. It's not a fairy tale, although I sometimes wish it were. The last time I saw the band play was when they were just starting out. It seems like it only happened yesterday. We were young then and would spend all day just dreaming of the things we would do and the people we would become later. During that summer, the band had formed. Most of them knew a few chords only. One day they would all become musical geniuses, but for now they were just a bunch of teens that had not yet bloomed into their full potential. Many months later, they had finally cut their first LP (that's what people listened to around 1969), and were touring for weeks on end. At first, it seemed like a dream, but that would soon change. By the time they reached 30, they had done it all, seen it all and wanted no more. They felt like they had already done everything they could and there was nothing new to discover. People were still buying their records, but how long would it last? Before they became "has-beens," they decided to put an end to it.

Last week, I saw an ad in the local paper. They were getting together for one final show (or so it seems). Yesterday, I got a call from one of the guys. They want me back in the band. Next month, we're hitting the road one last time. No matter how old we are, I guess we still have rock and roll in our soul.

ACTIVITY 3 — Above and Beyond

1. **Write five sentences describing how different types of music make you feel. Use at least one adverb of manner, frequency, intensity or degree in each sentence.**

2. **Underline or highlight the adverbs in each sentence.**

Example: Classical music makes me feel <u>rather</u> sleepy.

a) _____
b) _____
c) _____
d) _____
e) _____

Name: _____ Date: _____ Group: _____

Prepositions

*When did you hear them play **for** the last time?* ❶

*Really, where have they gone **since** then?* ❸

*It was back **in** 1969. They were **on** the top of the charts **at** the time.* ❷

*They moved **to** England after Woodstock. That was a long time ago.* ❹

Focus on…

Prepositions of Time

in: used with months, seasons, years, time of day and periods of time
   Examples: **in** January, **in** 1978, **in** the 20s

on: used with days of the week and specific dates
   Examples: **on** Monday, **on** October 23, **on** Christmas Day

at: used with precise time
   Example: **at** six o'clock

for: used to express duration
   Examples: **for** three weeks, **for** ten minutes, **for** two months

during: used with a noun to express when something happened
   Examples: **during** the Civil War, **during** the show

since: used to show when the action began (specific days, months, years or dates)
   Example: **since** May 12, 2004

For telling time…
*It's ten **to** seven. (6:50)*
*It's half **past** four. (4:30)*

⚠️ **PAY ATTENTION!**

NB: We say: "in the morning," "in the afternoon," "in the evening" but "**at night**."

Practise!

1. Highlight the prepositions of time in the following text.

We usually met after work at Jack's home. We would stay there between five-thirty and seven o'clock. We usually left after supper and came back for a few hours. We would finally leave by four o'clock in the morning. During that time, we practised and learned a great number of songs which we have since forgotten. But that was a long time ago. I can't stay up until sunrise anymore.

2. Put the appropriate preposition in the following sentences

   a) It was exactly twelve o'clock and the show was scheduled to start _____ midnight.

   b) _____ New Year's Day, the tickets were put on sale.

   c) We were now _____ June.

   d) I had waited for this show _____ six months.

---

40 | Unit 2 ■ Tuning In! | Thank you for not photocopying. | © Éditions Grand Duc

Focus on...

Prepositions of Location and Direction

Prepositions of location

Examples:

The socks are **on** the floor.
The basket is **under (underneath)** the desk.
The light switch is **above (over)** the nightstand.
The stereo is **between** the speakers.
The dresser is **in front of** the window.
The pillow is **behind (in back of)** the bear.
The desk is **across from** the dresser.

The guitar is **against** the wall.
The alarm clock is **next to** the lamp.
The hockey stick is **near (close to)** the guitar.
The computer screen is **far from** the window.
The pencils are **to the left of** the screen.
The books are **to the right of** the telephone.

Prepositions to show direction

Examples:

across (over to the other side): I swam **across** the lake.
into (entering a place or building): He went **into** the store.
onto (up on the top of something): She threw it **onto** the pile of clothes.
through (in one side and out the other): He drove **through** the tunnel.
towards (in the direction of): We walked **towards** the crowd.

ACTIVITY 4

Choose the appropriate prepositions from the Word Bank to complete the sentences.

a) He was in such a hurry that he crashed _____ the screen door.

b) He used to travel _____ Farnham and Montreal every day.

c) She was sitting _____ me at the concert when I first noticed her.

d) He was always _____ to his mother as a child.

e) He lived _____ the Inuit for a year.

f) He lives _____ Spain for six months every year.

g) He has an apartment _____ Saint-Laurent Boulevard.

h) That rabbit dug a hole _____ the fence to get to my garden.

i) He lives in an apartment _____ mine.

j) The office is situated _____ 1000 Main Street.

Word Bank

- in
- on
- at
- under
- through
- between
- above
- beside
- close
- among

Name: _____ Date: _____ Group: _____

Focus on...

Prepositions of Manner

Prepositions of manner help you describe **how actions are completed**.

The most common prepositions of manner are:
- **by:** He learned to play **by** ear.
- **in:** He writes his songs **in** green ink.
- **like:** He plays the guitar **like** a wild man.
- **with:** He composes **with** passion.

ACTIVITY 5 — Above and Beyond

Complete the puzzle and find the mystery words. Choose from all types of prepositions.

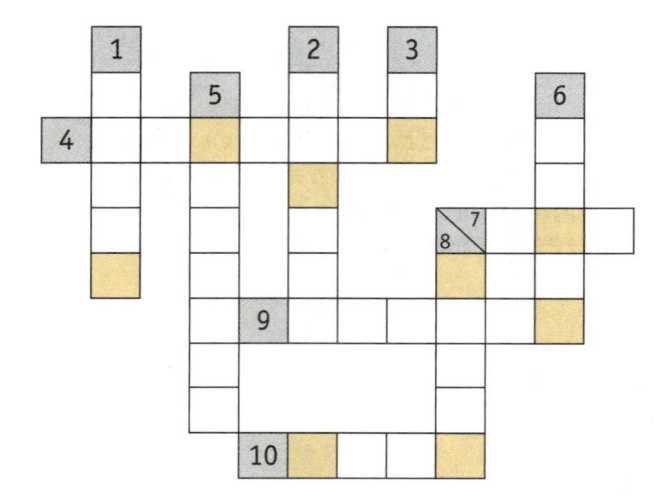

__ __ __ __ __ SMALL WORDS GO A __ __ __ __ WAY.

ACROSS

4. I always played _____ the bassist and lead guitar.
7. We toured with the group _____ three years.
9. We still get together and jam _____ summer holidays.
10. He plays the guitar _____ Chuck Berry.

DOWN

1. The recording studio is two floors _____ my apartment.
2. The drummer is always placed _____ the rest of the group.
3. We would usually practise _____ Mondays.
5. At the end of the set, he put his foot _____ the bass drum.
6. An aria by Mozart was found _____ some old newspapers.
8. The group hasn't played together _____ 2001.

42 Unit 2 ■ Tuning In! Thank you for not photocopying. © Éditions Grand Duc

ACTIVITY 6 — Above and Beyond

Choose the appropriate prepositions and adverbs from the Word Bank to complete the text. They may be used more than once.

Word Bank

- along
- accurately
- always
- among
- at
- by
- closer to
- frequently
- from
- in
- normally
- now
- of
- on
- once
- perfectly
- still
- to
- today
- with

Rolling Stone

When I was a teenager back _____ the early 70s, a song made popular _____ Dr. Hook and the Medicine Show described a magazine which reflected my generation. The song was entitled "Cover of the Rolling Stone." This magazine created _____ 1967 _____ two young men, Jann Wenner and Ralph J. Gleason, _____ reflected the mentality _____ the time. It _____ reported _____ the musical culture _____ the era. _____ the bands and singers to grace its cover were the Grateful Dead, the Beatles, Jimi Hendrix, Janis Joplin, Bob Dylan and many, many more. To appear _____ the cover _____ Rolling Stone magazine was synonymous _____ success.

The magazine did not only report _____ music (although it was _____ its major interest), it very _____ reported on the hot topics of the day. The Vietnam War, feminism, abortion and gay rights were _____ the many causes championed by the magazine. _____, music and movies were the main staples of Rolling Stone _____ with art and photography. Many photographers who worked _____ Rolling Stone went on to become very famous.

But as the baby boomers, its main audience, went _____ teenagers _____ adults _____ middle age, so did the magazine. _____ the mid 80s, it had become more institutionalized, and topics it _____ would have rejected, it now printed. Its advertisements also reflected this reality. Where it _____ advertised different brands of cigarette paper, it _____ advertised luxury cars. Also _____ that time, it had moved its operations _____ San Francisco _____ New York to be _____ major advertising firms. _____, the magazine is _____ owned _____ one of the original founders, Jan Wenner, who also owns Wenner Media.

Name: _____   Date: _____   Group: _____

Continuous Verb Tenses

① What **are** you **doing**?

② **I'm reading** an article about the show we saw last night.

③ Why **are** you **reading** the article? You were there.

④ I just want to see what the newspapers **are saying** about it.

⑤ So, what **are** they **saying**?

Focus on...

The Present Continuous Tense

The present continuous tense is used for:
- an action that is taking place now
- an action that will take place in the future

How to form it:
Use **to be** in the **present tense** and add **-ing** to the **base form of the verb**.
Example: He **is rehearsing** for tonight's show.

Keywords
- now
- at this moment
- Listen!
- right now
- currently
- Look!

Negative form:
For the negative form of the present continuous, add **not** between the auxiliary and the main verb.
Examples: He **is not tuning** his guitar.
He **isn't practising** the last song.

Interrogative form:
- **Yes/No questions: auxiliary + subject + verb**
Example: **Are** they **getting** ready to go onstage?
- **Information questions:**
question word + auxiliary + subject + verb
Example: When **is** the show **starting**?

NB: The present continuous is usually used with action verbs, not stative verbs. The following verbs cannot be conjugated in the present continuous form: **like, love, hate, want, wish, believe, belong, need, own, seem, know, mean, remember, understand.**

Practise!

Put the verbs in parentheses in the present continuous tense.

a) John (to listen) to his favourite band.
_____

b) I (to begin) to understand why he likes that group.
_____

c) We (to take, question) a bus to go to the show.
_____

d) The show (start, neg.) as scheduled.
_____

44 Unit 2 ■ Tuning In!   Thank you for not photocopying.   © Éditions Grand Duc

Name: _____ Date: _____ Group: _____

ACTIVITY 7

Put the verbs in parentheses in the simple present or present continuous tense.

That's Good Music!

I (to sit) _____ here in my living room and I (to listen) _____ to a beautiful piece of music. It (to be) _____ not a classical piece in the sense that some people might (to interpret) _____ it. You (to know) _____ it (to be) _____ classical if it (to have) _____ the name Beethoven or Mozart written on it. By classical, I (to mean) _____ a piece of music that (to resist) _____ the test of time. Something that you will listen to in 20, 30, 40 or even 50 years and (to say) _____, "Now that was good music!" or "They (to write, neg.) _____ them like that anymore!" Naturally, we all (to have) _____ different tastes in music. Even within the same generation, people's tastes (to diverge) _____, so (to imagine) _____ between several generations.

You (to say, probably) _____ to yourselves, "What (to know, question) _____ about good music?" Well, I (to know) _____ a lot. I (to listen) _____ to different styles of music, from Beethoven to the latest sounds on the charts. I (to like, neg., always) _____ what I (to hear) _____ but at least, I (to keep) _____ an open mind. That (to be) _____ what you should also (to do) _____. I (to imply, neg.) _____ you should (to spend) _____ hours concentrating on Beethoven's Ninth or Brahm's Lullaby. I (to suggest, neg., even) _____ that you (to play) _____ the music for one whole hour, but (to give) _____ yourself the chance to say, "I listened and I didn't like it." Then again, who (to know) _____, you might actually (to enjoy) _____ it. By the way, the piece of classical music I (to savour) _____ at this moment (to be) _____ "Yesterday" by the Beatles. They have passed the test of time. Almost 50 years later, people (to sing, still) _____ their songs. That (to be) _____ truly a classic.

ACTIVITY 8

Change the following sentences into information questions.

a) They are playing tomorrow.

_____

b) She is singing well.

_____

c) John is accompanying her on the guitar.

_____

d) John is also singing along with Evelyne.

_____

e) They are recording a very beautiful song.

_____

Name: _____ Date: _____ Group: _____

① Do you remember what you **were doing** when you heard the news?

② Yeah, I **was reading** a book. What about you?

③ I **was driving** back from work.

④ Just imagine our kid brother's first record. Makes you want to cry.

Focus on...

The Past Continuous Tense

The past continuous tense is used for:
- an action that was going on **in the past**
- two **simultaneous actions**

Keywords
during, when, while, as, etc.

How to form it:

Use the verb **to be** in the **past tense** and add **-ing** to the **base form** of the verb.

Examples: I **was watching** television when he came in with the good news.
I **was listening** to Beethoven on my favourite radio station while I was eating.

Negative form:

Add **not** between the auxiliary **to be** and the **main verb**.

Examples: I **was not eating** when you called.
They **were not watching** television when they received the news.
He **wasn't listening** to the demo tape when she arrived.

Interrogative form:

- **Yes/No questions:** auxiliary + subject + verb

Example: **Were** they **doing** a sound check when the microphone broke?

- **Information questions:** question word + auxiliary + subject + verb

Example: What **were** they **practising** when she arrived?

Unit 2 ■ Tuning In!

ACTIVITY 9

1. Write a sentence describing each picture on the lines below.
2. In each sentence, use a verb in the simple past and one in the past continuous tense.
   NB: The verb that interrupts the action should be in the past tense.

Example: I was studying when the phone rang./He was studying when the phone rang.

UNIT 2 — Wrap-up

ACTIVITY A

Put the verbs in parentheses in the simple past or the past continuous tense.

The Encyclopedia of Rock and Roll

Last Sunday, I (to visit) _____ old man Burns. He (to read) _____ from a book when I (to show up) _____. The book (to seem) _____ to be an encyclopedia of some sort. He (to go, slowly) _____ down each page and (to smile) _____. A little boy (to sit) _____ next to him. I (to recognize) _____ the boy; he (to be) _____ old man Burns' grandson. The little boy (to look) _____ at his grandfather with admiring eyes. He (to be) _____ truly (to captivate) _____ by what the old man (to say) _____. As I (to approach) _____ them, the old man (to raise) _____ his head and (to smile) _____ at me.

"Well, hello," he (to say) _____, "what brings you here today?"

"Oh nothing," I (to answer) _____, "I (to pass, just) _____ by and I (to decide) _____ to stop and see how you (to be) _____."

"I am fine, as you can see. Do you know my grandson Tommy?"

"Not really," I (to reply) _____. "Hi, Tommy."

The little boy (to look) _____ up and (to smile) _____ but (to keep) _____ quiet.

"Tommy is a bit shy," old man Burns (to continue) _____.

"I see," I (to say) _____. "What (to read) _____ when I (to arrive) _____?"

Old man Burns (to turn) _____ the book around and (to show) _____ me the cover. It (to be) _____ the *Encyclopedia of Rock and Roll*.

"I (to go) _____ through the passage that (to mention) _____ my band."

"You (to be) _____ in a band?" I (to ask) _____, surprised. "A real rock and roll band?"

"We (to be) _____ on our last road trip when I (to quit) _____."

"Why?" I (to gasp) _____. I couldn't understand why someone would give up a life of music in a rock and roll band just like that.

Old man Burns simply (to wink) _____ and (to whisper) _____, "I (to meet) _____ Tommy's grandmother, (to fall) _____ in love and (to decide) _____ to get (to marry) _____. And besides, because the band (to break) _____ up for no apparent reason, I (to end) _____ the adventure on an air of mystery. That's why we are in this encyclopedia."

Name: _____ Date: _____ Group: _____

ACTIVITY B

1 In the following text, put the verbs in parentheses in the simple present, simple past or the present or past continuous tense.

2 Fill in the blanks with the correct adverb (A) or preposition (P) from the Word Bank or with the appropriate subject or object pronouns (Pr).

Orpheus and Eurydice

Orpheus was a musician who (to play) _____ the lyre. (Pr) _____ was (A) _____ good that even the trees, animals, rocks and rivers (to come) _____ to listen to (Pr) _____. One day, as (Pr) _____ (to play) _____ the lyre, he (to meet) _____ a beautiful nymph, Eurydice, and he (to fall) _____ in love with (Pr) _____. Soon (P) _____ their marriage, Eurydice was bitten by a snake and (to die) _____. Orpheus was (A) _____ heartbroken, so one day, (Pr) _____ (to decide) _____ to go to Hades, to fetch his beloved. (P) _____ some searching, he (to reach) _____ the throne of Pluto and Proserpine, the King and Queen of the Underworld. He (to sing) _____ for (Pr) _____ with his harp. His music was (A) _____ beautiful that even the ghosts (to weep) _____. Pluto at long last, said, "Go quickly, take her, (Pr) _____ shall walk (P) _____ (Pr) _____ but don't look back (P) _____ her. If you (to look) _____ (P) _____ (Pr) _____ before she (to reach) _____ the land of light, she will return (P) _____ (Pr) _____." Orpheus (to turn) _____ and quickly (to leave) _____ Hades. As he (to walk) _____, (Pr) _____ (to listen) _____, but he (to hear) _____ nothing (P) _____ him. "Perhaps the King and Queen (to try) _____ to deceive (Pr) _____," he (to think) _____. "Maybe I (to lose) _____ her again." (Pr) _____ kept on walking and (A) _____ he could see the light of the upper world. (Pr) _____ was (A) _____ excited that he (to turn) _____ to embrace Eurydice. He heard (Pr) _____ cry. (Pr) _____ (to see) _____ her as (P) _____ a mist and then, she (to dissolve) _____ (P) _____ smoke. When (Pr) _____ returned (P) _____ Earth, his sadness turned to despair. His music (to become) _____ (A) _____ beautiful, as (Pr) _____ (to sing) _____ for his lost Eurydice. (A) _____, he (to retire) _____ to a cave. Men and women (to come) _____ to him to listen to his music, but he (to drive) _____ them all away. One day, (A) _____ women, infuriated by Orpheus' rejection of them, fell on (Pr) _____ and killed him. As a ghost, he returned (P) _____ Hades, and was (A) _____ reunited with Eurydice. After Orpheus' death, Zeus took his harp and set (Pr) _____ among the stars. He called it Lyra, and it is still there today.

Refer to Chapter 1 for help with pronouns.

Word Bank

Adverbs
- completely
- finally
- hauntingly
- several
- so
- soon

Prepositions
- after
- at
- behind
- like
- to
- through

UNIT 3 — On the Edge

Punctuation

Focus on...

Punctuation Marks

Punctuation marks are signals to the reader. They help make the message clearer.

Sometimes, the meaning of a sentence can change completely depending on the punctuation.

Punctuation Mark	When to Use It	Examples
Period (.)	• To indicate the end of a complete sentence	• My passion is hiking. • He is an excellent skier.
Question mark (?)	• To indicate a question	• Where are you going?
Exclamation mark (!)	• To indicate surprise or strong emotion	• Wow! I can't believe you won! • That's fantastic!
Apostrophe (')	• In contractions • To show possession	• They don't want to take a taxi before seven o'clock. • Jane's phone number • The Smiths' address
Hyphen (-)	• To make compound words • To write compound numbers • To join prefixes to words	• rip-off • twenty-seven, seventy-seven • mini-series, anti-social, semi-colon

ACTIVITY 1

Insert the appropriate punctuation (period, question mark, exclamation mark, apostrophe or hyphen) in the following sentences.

a) They were stranded on a tiny island in the middle of the lake The temperature had dropped to minus twenty five degrees Celsius

b) They held on for dear life They didn t want to fall asleep

c) The question on everyone s mind was: How were they going to get out of there

d) Did they know survival techniques or were they relying on luck

e) Some thought they weren t getting out alive Others still kept hoping, no matter what

f) Twenty four hours later, there was still no sign of any rescue party

g) Their hopes were revived when an airplane s engine was heard in the distance

Name: _____ Date: _____ Group: _____

Focus on...

More Punctuation Marks

> There is no comma after the next-to-last item.

Punctuation Mark	When to Use It	Examples
Comma (,)	• To separate items in a list	• Please buy cheese, eggs, milk and bread.
	• To separate two phrases	• Before you leave, please turn off the lights.
	• After introductory words	• Dear John, I will do it tomorrow.
	• To separate adjectives	• The mountain climber wore thick, woollen socks.
	• Before coordinating conjunctions: *and, but, for, or, so, yet*	• I knew the terrain was a challenge, so I took my GPS.
	• To set off interjections and the words *Yes* and *No*	• Well, I think we must help him. • Yes, Marianne was there.
	• To address someone	• Sir, can you tell me where I might find a phone?
	• For appositions	• The girl, a former athlete, was able to survive because of her stamina.
Colon (:)	• To introduce a list of items	• This is what you need: a sleeping bag, a pillow, an extra blanket and warm clothes.
	• In a business letter greeting	• Dear Madam:
	• In time	• 8:15 p.m.
Semi-colon (;)	• To join related sentences into one sentence	• I told him not to go; it is too dangerous.
	• For lists that already have commas in them	• They toured: Toronto, ON; Montreal, QC; Halifax, NS and Moncton, NB.

ACTIVITY 2

Insert the appropriate punctuation (comma, colon or semi-colon) in the following sentences.

a) When going into the wilderness here are a few items you might want to take along matches a flashlight a compass a map of the region and some common sense.

b) My friend an avid fan of camping got lost one day.

c) He started out from Gray Creek BC headed northwest toward Nelson and lost his way.

d) He never got over that experience it haunted him all his life.

e) Actually we never did let him forget.

Focus on...

Quotation Marks

Quotation marks are used as punctuation in order to quote a person's exact words when they are incorporated into a text.

Using other punctuation with quotation marks:

Punctuation	Examples
Use a **comma** to introduce the quotation.	• The pilot said, "That looks like a smoke signal."
Put **commas** and **periods** <u>inside</u> quotation marks.	• "We were stuck in the elevator for 12 hours before help came." • "We found them," was all he said.
Put **question marks** and **exclamation marks**: – <u>inside</u> quotation marks when they are part of the quotation – <u>outside</u> when they are not	• "Wow! That's incredible!" he exclaimed. "Where did you hear that?" • Is it about the "urban jungle"?

ACTIVITY 3

Insert the appropriate punctuation in the following sentences.

a) She said   Look out   The roof is about to cave in

b)   Quick Come to the cellar We ll be safe there

c)   Be careful   she said as they ran downstairs   the lights just went out

d) The tornado roared outside   while inside a little voiced cried   We re going to die

e)   No we re not   her mother said   Everything will be all right

f) The tornado finally roared off into the distance   It s over   she said. We re alive

g)   What are you so happy about   asked Tommy

h) Jim looked surprised as he answered   I still can t believe we made it

i) Tommy wasn t smiling   We were lucky this time

j)   Well luck or no luck the tornado passed and we re still here

ACTIVITY 4 — Above and Beyond

Insert the appropriate punctuation in the following text.

Boy Survives Mountain Lion Attack
By Mike Celizic

Paul John Schalow is a 10 year old who loves riding ATVs in the wilds of Arizona and he s not going to stop just because the last time he went he was attacked by a rabid mountain lion

P J as he s known looked none the worse for wear on Wednesday in New York when he told Today s Matt Lauer about the attack which happened last Saturday while he was on a family outing in Arizona s Tonto National Forest

Ten adults were on the expedition along with P J who was celebrating his birthday and his cousin Brittany 9

After a morning spent riding their ATVs they stopped by a river around 2 p m to eat lunch The two kids were on a sandy beach when the female mountain lion arrived apparently also intent on a meal

She was walking and she just stopped right behind me P J said his tone as matter of fact as if he were describing an encounter with a kitten I see my little cousin Brittany She looks scared in her face So I turn around and I see it Then everyone starts saying 'Hold still Hold still ' so we just froze

I was actually scared at first I was shaking added Brittany who said her discomfort was made worse because she had an itch in her back

But when she heard her grandmother yelling Stay still Don t move Don t move that s just what she did

P J s grandfather Newton Smith was about 10 feet away and he s convinced that had the children started screaming and running the lion would have gone into lethal attack mode Instead it casually investigated P J who showed remarkable courage by standing stock still as the animal scratched his back with its claws Even when the lion opened its jaws and tried to get his head in its jaws he didn t move

Source: Mike Celizic, "Boy keeps cool as mountain lion tries to eat him", *Today Show*, March 12, 2008 [online].

ACTIVITY 5

Complete the crossword puzzle on punctuation and find the mystery message!

ACROSS

1. One use for an apostrophe.
6. The punctuation mark that ends this sentence: "What's the problem"
7. Punctuate the following sentence: "All I can say is: wow"
9. What is missing in the following sentence: "You must bring the following warm boots, a warm sweater and a tuque."
10. Shows possession.
12. Mark used when repeating someone's words.
13. Puts an end to it.
14. Used with compound numbers.

DOWN

2. A comma goes before coordinating one of these.
3. What a hyphen will join to words.
4. What is missing in the following sentence: "Our expedition will take us to Lima, Peru Santiago, Chile and Buenos Aires, Argentina."
5. Separates items in a list.
8. In the sentence: "Jacques, my very good friend, climbs mountains for fun," what is the expression **"my very good friend"** called?
11. What an exclamation mark shows.

Name: _____ Date: _____ Group: _____

Punctuation gives rhythm to your _ _ _ _ _ _ _ _ _ .

Unit 3 ■ On the Edge

Perfect and Conditional Verb Tenses

① Where **have you been** for the past two weeks?

③ Did it go well?

⑤ And how was it the last time.

② Hiking. I hiked the Appalachian Trail.

④ Yeah! It was nothing new. I**'ve done** it before.

⑥ The same. It was as if I**'d never left** the place.

Focus on...

The Present Perfect Tense

The **present perfect tense** is used for an action that is finished but has a direct link with the present. There is more action to come.

How to form it:

Use **to have** in the **present tense** and add the **past participle** of the verb.

Examples: Daniel **has climbed** Mount Jacques-Cartier many times.
The students **have learned** speleology.

Keywords
- already
- since
- ever
- until now
- so far
- up to now
- not yet
- many times
- yet
- for

Negative form:

For the negative form, add **NOT** between the **auxiliary** and the **past participle**.

Examples: She **has not seen** them.
They **haven't completed** their work.

Interrogative form:

- Yes/No questions:
auxiliary + subject + past participle

Example: **Has he left** yet?

- Information questions:
question word + auxiliary + subject + past participle

Example: Where **have they gone**?

Practise!

Write the verbs in parentheses in the present perfect tense.

a) He (to read) _____ many stories about survival.

b) They (to teach) _____ a survival course for many years now.

c) We (to draw, already) _____ our itinerary for our hiking trip.

d) She (to live) _____ through many exciting adventures.

e) I see you (to study, neg.) _____ astronomy.

f) Yes, it will be useful when I'm on the trip I (to plan) _____.

g) (to write, you, question) _____ many possible scenarios for your trip so far?

h) Not just for this trip. It is something I (to do) _____ every time up to now.

Unit 3 ■ On the Edge

Name: _____ Date: _____ Group: _____

ACTIVITY 6

1 Unscramble the following words to make complete sentences or questions.

a) many – climbed – mountains – has – she?
_____

b) Everest – not – of – to – they – have – top – the – been.
_____

c) Johnson – have – book – you – read – mountains – by – on – the?
_____

d) prepare – time – have – yet – we – had – not – to.
_____

e) guiding – I – him – have – us – spoken – to – about.
_____

f) Nepal – you – been – have – yet – to?
_____

g) top – the – sick – no one – been – so – climbing – has – to – far.
_____

h) expedition – have – you – many – learned – on – this – things?
_____

2 a) Unscramble the following words to make complete sentences.
   b) Then rewrite the sentence in the negative contracted form.

   1) as – for – he – many – has – a – worked – guide – years.
   _____
   _____

   2) before – we – that – have – made – climb.
   _____
   _____

   3) have – on – Rouge – before – they – the – River – rafted.
   _____
   _____

   4) next – plane – they – reserved – have – tickets – their – for – year.
   _____
   _____

© Éditions Grand Duc   Thank you for not photocopying.   Unit 3 ▪ On the Edge   57

Name: _____ Date: _____ Group: _____

Focus on...

Choosing Between the Simple Past and the Present Perfect

1. Is the action finished?
   ↓
   Yes
   ↓
2. Is the moment specified?
   ↓   ↓
   Yes   No
   ↓   ↓
   Simple Past   **Present Perfect**
   ↑   ↑
   No   Yes

Is there more to follow soon?

⚠️ **PAY ATTENTION!**
Check pp. 20 and 56 to review keywords for the simple past tense and the present perfect tense.

You may also need the past continuous. The past continuous tense is used for actions in the past that were going on when something else interrupted them.

Example: He was floating on the icy water when the rescue squad found him.

---

since vs. for

- Use **since** with the present perfect to show when a first action started.

Examples: He has been a paramedic since 1998.
He has not hiked up that mountain since he sprained his ankle.

- Use **for** to show the duration of an action.

Examples: He has been a paramedic for seven years.
He has been in a hospital for two months.
(He is still there.)

Practise!

Write the verbs in parentheses in the present perfect or the simple past tense.

A Walk in the Forest

Yesterday, my friends (to take) _____ a long walk in the forest. It (to be) _____ a long time since they (to walk) _____ through it. It (to seem) _____ deserted to them, but in reality, it (to hide) _____ a great quantity of organisms. So far, my explorer friends (to see, not really) _____ all the beauty it hides. All they (to notice) _____ were the dangers it (to exhibit) _____.

They (to realize, not yet) _____ that its beauty (to exist) _____ for a much longer time than its dangers.

58 Unit 3 • On the Edge

Name: _____ Date: _____ Group: _____

ACTIVITY 7

a) For each of the following sentences, put a check mark if the verbs are conjugated correctly.
b) If they are incorrect, write the correct form in the column marked "Correction."

	OK	Correction
1) I studied map reading since I was 10.		
2) They climbed Kilimanjaro a few years ago.		
3) He has rafted almost every river in Quebec so far.		
4) I have seen a skydiving competition last week.		
5) The expedition did not leave the base camp yet.		
6) My friend went down to the *Empress of Ireland* last month.		
7) He has always liked a challenge such as swimming the rapids.		
8) He swam the Chambly rapids three times already.		
9) Up to now, there have been no serious injuries in the Chambly rapids.		
10) They participated in rafting competitions for the last 10 years.		
11) Last year, he has gone down the Colorado River.		
12) I have not yet tried bungee jumping.		
13) Did you ever drive a Formula One car?		
14) He has piloted a glider for the first time last weekend.		
15) He scaled El Capitan five years ago.		

Name: _____ Date: _____ Group: _____

① *What happened to the expedition?*

② People **had already left** the base camp when the storm started.

③ *Why didn't they come back to the base camp?*

④ They **had lost** all sense of direction by that time. All they could do was sit the storm out.

⑤ **Had they listened** to the weather report before taking off, they would have saved themselves a lot of trouble.

Focus on...

The Past Perfect Tense

The **past perfect tense** is used for an action in the past that happened before another one.

How to form it:

Use **to have** in the **past tense** and add the **past participle** of the verb.

Example: They **had already left** when Marina arrived.

Keywords
- already
- before
- once
- until then
- by that time
- never
- not yet

Negative form:

For the negative form, add **NOT** between the **auxiliary** and the **past participle**.

Examples: Barbara **had not seen** him.
Barbara **hadn't seen** him.

Interrogative form:

- **Yes/No questions:** auxiliary + subject + past participle

Example: **Had he received** a warning?

- **Information questions:**
question word + auxiliary + subject + past participle

Example: When **had he received** the warning?

Practise!

Write the verbs in parentheses in the past perfect tense.

a) The ski patrol (to give, neg.) _____ everyone on the slope any warning of imminent danger.

b) The avalanche (to be) _____ predicted.

c) Still, it (to take) _____ some skiers by surprise.

d) Those who (to make) _____ the mistake of not taking the warning seriously were in potential danger.

e) (to go, they) _____ off the beaten trail and far from safety?

f) Yes, and it is clear they (to act) _____ irresponsibly.

g) They (to risk) _____ their lives and those of others.

Name: _____ Date: _____ Group: _____

ACTIVITY 8

Rewrite the following sentences in the interrogative form (Yes/No questions) and the negative form.

a) The firemen had looked everywhere for victims before leaving the scene.

Interrogative form: _____

Negative form: _____

b) The airplane had crashed right after takeoff.

I.: _____

N.: _____

c) The pilot had already received the wrong information.

I.: _____

N.: _____

d) The control tower had made a serious mistake.

I.: _____

N.: _____

e) The controller had seen another plane on the radar before.

I.: _____

N.: _____

f) An incident like this had happened once before.

I.: _____

N.: _____

ACTIVITY 9

Write the verbs in parentheses in the past perfect or the simple past tense.

a) The incident (to take) _____ place in August 1959.

b) Until then, Marine pilot William Rankin (to see, never) _____ such a storm.

c) As he (to fly) _____ into the storm, his jet fighter engine (to stop, suddenly) _____.

d) Because of the danger, at 16,000 metres he (to bail out) _____ and (to drop) _____ into the heart of the storm below him.

e) His parachute (to open) _____ just as he (to enter) _____ the storm.

f) Instantly, black, grey and white clouds (to surround) _____ him.

g) He (to feel) _____ like he (to drop) _____ into a washing machine.

h) His body (to twist) _____ and (to turn) _____ like a rag doll.

i) He (to want, neg.) _____ to see anything so he (to keep) _____ his eyes shut.

j) It (to seem) _____ that his body (to be) _____ just a bag of bones being (to smash) _____ on a cement wall.

k) He (to fall) _____ in an irregular pattern. Sometimes the storm (to lift) _____ him up before it (to drop) _____ him again.

l) When he (to pass, finally) _____ through the clouds, he (to be) _____ only 100 metres from the ground.

m) Luckily, at the end, a tree (to break) _____ his fall.

n) Surprisingly, the fall (to injure, neg.) _____ his body. He (to suffer, only) _____ from shock and frostbite.

Name: _____ Date: _____ Group: _____

ACTIVITY 10 **Above and Beyond**

Choose the past perfect, past continuous or simple past tense to complete the following text. Circle the correct answer.

News Report

Reporter: Here we are on the corner of Mann and 22nd Avenue where a fire (was/has been/was being) raging for the past three hours. The cause of the blaze is still unknown, but in all evidence it (started/has started/was starting) in the basement of this three-storey building. We have with us a woman who (witnessed/has witnessed/was witnessing) everything up to now. Good afternoon, madam.

Woman: Good afternoon.

Reporter: May I ask what is your name and where do you live?

Woman: My name is Francine and I live right across the street.

Reporter: What (did you do/had you done/were you doing) when you first (saw/had seen/were seeing) the fire?

Francine: I (walked/had walked/was walking) my dog Daisy when she (started/had started/was starting) to bark and pull me toward this house. I (did not notice/had not noticed/was not noticing) anything strange until then. Suddenly, the windows in the basement (blew/had blown/were blowing) out. First, smoke (started/had started/was starting) to come out of the house and then flames.

Reporter: What (did you do/had you done/were you doing) then?

Francine: I (took/had taken/was taking) out my cellphone and (dialed/had dialed/was dialing) 911.

Reporter: How long (did it take/had it taken/was it taking) the fire department to respond?

Francine: Actually, it (took/had taken/was taking) a long time. It seems they (never were/had never been/were never being) in this part of the city before.

Reporter: What (happened/had happened/was happening) while they (were/had been/were being) on their way?

Francine: Well, people (left/had left/were leaving) the building as everything around them (fell/had fallen/was falling). It (reminded/had reminded/was reminding) me of something I (saw once/had once seen/was once seeing) on television about the *Hindenburg* disaster.

Reporter: Did everybody leave the building?

Francine: I don't know. The firemen (did not yet go/had not yet gone/were not yet going) inside the building when we (started/had started/were starting) talking.

Reporter: Thank you very much, madam. Now back to our studios for an update on sports.

© Éditions Grand Duc   Thank you for not photocopying.   Unit 3 ■ On the Edge

Name: _____   Date: _____   Group: _____

① *What **would** you do if you were left alone on an island?*

② *I **would** relax.*

③ *Then what **would** you do?*

④ *I **would** build a fire, make some kind of shelter, cook a steak dinner, watch TV. I don't know.*

⑤ *You obviously don't.*

Focus on...

The Conditional Tense

When to use the conditional tense:

- To talk about hypothetical choices (choices that may or may not be possible)
- For actions that could be done only under certain conditions

*Example: I **would call** the ski patrol if I had my cellphone with me.*

How to form it:

- Affirmative: **would** + verb (base form)   *Example: We **would take** a first-aid kit.*
- Negative: **wouldn't** + verb (base form)   *Example: I **wouldn't go** alone.*
- Interrogative: **would** + subject + verb (base form)   *Example: **Would you travel** alone?*

Note

After **if**, use the **past tense** (not the conditional).

*Examples: If they **went** camping, they would take a first-aid kit.*
*If I **had** a dog, I would take him with me for safety.*
*I wouldn't go hiking if I **were** not fit.*

⚠️ **PAY ATTENTION!**

In an "if-clause," the verb *to be* takes the form *were*.

*Example: If I **were** a better skier, I'd go skiing in the Rockies.*

Practise!

1. Write the verbs in parentheses in the conditional tense.

a) If they went on a trek, they (to have) _____ a lot of material to buy.

b) I (to need) _____ warm clothes, if I hiked during the winter.

c) If you wanted to climb Everest, you (to practise) _____ on other challenging peaks first.

d) If I were to sail across the ocean, I (to learn) _____ about navigation first.

e) (to come, you, question) _____ with me on a trip to Spain?

f) I (to accept, certainly) _____ such a gracious invitation.

Unit 3 ■ On the Edge

2. Answer the following questions with a complete sentence in the affirmative or the negative form.

Example: What would you do if you had a million dollars?
If I had a million dollars, I would buy a motorcycle for my grandfather.
OR
If I had a million dollars, I wouldn't watch extreme sports on TV, I would practise them.

a) What would you do if you were lost in the woods?
_____

b) What would you do if you were caught in a fire?
_____

c) What would you do if someone you knew was in a burning house?
_____

d) What would you do if your ship went down?
_____

e) What would you do if you were in a traffic accident?
_____

ACTIVITY 11

Unscramble the following words to form sentences in the conditional tense.

a) caught – could – I – I – I – if – would – avalanche – run – as – as – were – an – in – fast.
_____

b) directions – if – ask – I – I – lost – would – in – city – strange – were – a – for.
_____

c) dead – a – play – I – if – attacked – me – bear – would – not.
_____

d) were – fire – on – build – would – a – if – island – I – I – an – stranded.
_____

e) water – jump – drowning – if – you – someone – would – in – him – to – saw – you – the – save?
_____

Name: _____ Date: _____ Group: _____

Focus on...

The Sequence of Verb Tenses

- The **present perfect** is a verb tense in the **past** that carries over to the **present**.
- The **present continuous** is a verb tense of the **present** that carries on into the **future**.
- The **past continuous** is a verb tense in the **past**. It is used for an action that was taking place when another event occured.

ACTIVITY 12

Use the verb "to report" in each example to complete the following chart.
You can refer to p. 132 of the Reference Section to help you.

Past	Present	Future
Simple past I _____ the results of last week's regatta.	**Simple present** He _____ everything that happens.	**Simple future** She _____ on the downhill race next weekend.
Past continuous I _____ on that boating accident when I fell in the river.		
Past perfect I _____ the story when he phoned.		

Present Perfect
They _____ the same tragic story many times.

Present Continuous
She _____ on the events.

Conditional
He _____ every detail if he could.

66 Unit 3 ■ On the Edge

ACTIVITY 13

Read the text and conjugate the verbs in parentheses. Choose between the simple present, the simple past, the present perfect, the present continuous and the conditional tense.

A Helping Hand

Throughout the ages, man (to witness) _____ many disasters, which (to put) _____ his strength and will to survive to the test. We (to have) _____ our share of disasters in Quebec. The one that (to stand out) _____ in our minds (to be) _____ the great ice storm of 1998. Many people (to remember) _____ that period as if it (to be) _____ yesterday.

A great number of people (to perform) _____ incredible acts of bravery and kindness. They (to take in) _____ friends and neighbours and at times, complete strangers. If you (to ask) _____ them what (to make) _____ them act the way they (to do) _____, the majority (to answer) _____ that they (to do) _____ nothing special. As it (to turn out) _____, many people who (to do) "_____ nothing special," (to put) _____ aside their personal well-being in order to help out others less fortunate. The rewards for their acts of humanity (to pay off, still) _____.

They (to create) _____ lifelong friendships with people they did not know. Those people now (to consider) _____ their friends as saviours and their saviours as friends.

A good friend of mine (to have) _____ the privilege of meeting a person he still (to call) _____ "friend."

Many (to do) _____ the same thing over if they (to have) _____ the chance. They (to extend) _____ a helping hand once again if there (to be) _____ another natural disaster like the one in 1998.

Unit 3 ■ On the Edge   67

Name: _____ Date: _____ Group: _____

UNIT 3 — Wrap-up

ACTIVITY A

Write the verbs in parentheses in the simple past, the past perfect, the past continuous or the conditional tense.

Surviving Our Teen Years (Part One)

When we get older and look back on our lives, we sometimes wonder how we (to manage) _____ to survive our teen years. When my friends and I (to be) _____ younger, we (to think, neg.) _____ we (to be) _____ mortal and because of this, we (to do) _____ extremely stupid things. We (to live) _____ on the edge. We (to look) _____ danger straight in the eye and (to flinch, neg.) _____. We (to consider) _____ death as something very far away and something that happened only to others. So, sit back and let me tell you how ignorant my friends and I (to be) _____ with regard to danger and immortality.

In the summer of '72, the town council (to hire) _____ about 20 teens to work on a government-funded project. Our job (to consist) _____ in cleaning the small river that passed through our town. They also (to tell) _____ us that we had to beautify the riverbanks. The first part of the job (to be) _____ a snap. We simply (to wade) _____ in the river and (to pick) _____ up anything that (to be, neg.) _____ naturally part of the river's ecosystem, such as tires, radiators, mufflers, hoods, and... well, you get the picture. The beautifying part of the job (to prove) _____ to be a bit more difficult. The plan (to consist) _____ in removing all the weeds along a certain stretch of the riverbank. We (to choose) _____ a particular spot on the river and (to make) _____ progress when someone (to come) _____ up with a brilliant idea. Why not build a stone wall along the river (or at least a section of it)? Great idea! The city council (to tell) _____ us they (to furnish) _____ a truck to carry the stones if we (to get) _____ a quarry to donate them. The quarry in a neighbouring city (to agree) _____ to participate. They (to donate) _____ the stones if we (to provide) _____ a truck to transport them. A win-win situation if ever we (to see) _____ one.

The following Monday, four of us (to arrive) _____ at the quarry for what proved to be a long, boring and life-changing job for us all. Our task (to be) _____ very simple: choose the biggest and flattest stones we could find, put them in a pile and wait for the truck to come and cart them off. The whole operation (to take) _____ four hours to perform on our part, but only 30 seconds on the part of the huge tractor to lift a shovel full of stones and dump them in the truck.

68 Unit 3 ■ On the Edge   Thank you for not photocopying.   © Éditions Grand Duc

ACTIVITY B

Write the verbs in parentheses in the simple past, the past perfect, the past continuous or the conditional tense.

Surviving Our Teen Years (Part Two)

By the second week, we (to begin) _____ to find the job somewhat repetitive and boring. What (to frustrate) _____ us most (to be, neg.) _____ the time it (to take) _____ to gather all the stones for one load, but the amount of time the tractor (to require) _____ to scoop up those long hours of work in the sun. As we (to discuss) _____ how easy it (to be) _____ if one of the quarry walls (to fall) _____, one of the guys (to point) _____ up and suddenly we (to realize) _____ we (to have) _____ our solution. At the very top of the wall (to hang) _____ a huge pile of rocks just waiting to fall. If that part of the wall (to tumble) _____, it (to solve) _____ all our problems. This (to be) _____ when "stupidity" (to show) _____ up. "It's easy," I (to say) _____. "All we have to do is climb up there and knock off the rocks holding that pile." Not any brighter, the rest of the group (to agree) _____. The only question that (to remain) _____ (to be) _____, "Who would climb to the top?" Maybe the sun (to shine) _____ too brightly, and it (to cloud) _____ any logical reasoning I had left. Whatever the reason, I (to decide) _____ to climb to the top. Since no one (to climb, ever) _____ besides me, I was the perfect choice.

When I (to reach) _____ the top, I slowly (to move) _____ under the overhanging pile of rocks to inspect the work to be done. I soon (to see) _____ that there were just a couple of big stones holding up the whole thing. I (to yell) _____ the good news down to the guys and they (to yell) _____ back to go for it and knock those rocks out of the way. As they (to shout) _____ their instructions, I (to hear) _____ another voice, not as loud as theirs, but very clear. For a few seconds, "stupidity" (to replace) _____ "common sense." But, when you are young and *immortal*, "stupidity" has a way of making sense. I (to decide) _____ to try and give a few kicks to the boulder that (to seem) _____ to hold the whole thing up. Suddenly, pebbles (to start) _____ falling on me and I (to jump) _____ out of the way just as everything (to come) _____ crashing down. When the dust (to settle, finally) _____, we (to see) _____ the results of our actions. I (to come) _____ within a few centimetres of going down with the pile; Jack (to hit) _____ by a small stone on the back of the head and still has the scar today; Yvon (to break) _____ his ankle as he (to run) _____ away from the avalanche. André (to make) _____ it to safety, but (to suffer) _____ from nightmares for a long time. What (to happen) _____ to the tractor parked at the foot of the cliff and our jobs? Total losses!

ACTIVITY C

Complete the crossword puzzle and find the mystery message.

ACROSS

1. Something which may or may not be possible is said to be _____.
5. The punctuation that goes at the end of the following sentence: "So, how are you doing" is a _____ mark.
8. Complete the sentence: They _____ seen Mount Everest before.
9. The suffix -ing added to the base form of a verb gives us a _____ tense.
11. An element of the perfect tense is a _____.
13. These punctuation marks are used when you want to quote someone.
15. Comma and coma _____ greatly in pronunciation and meaning.

DOWN

2. My students really surprised me. Although they never learned about _____, they knew exactly where to place a period or a colon in a text.
3. The word "twenty-seven" has one.
4. In a list, we use a _____ to separate the items.
6. Complete: If I _____ an adventurous person, I would hike the Appalachian Trail.
7. Modal used to express the conditional.
10. A keyword for the past perfect.
12. It marks the end of a sentence or an era in time.
14. "Until then" is a keyword used with the _____ perfect tense.

Name: _____ Date: _____ Group: _____

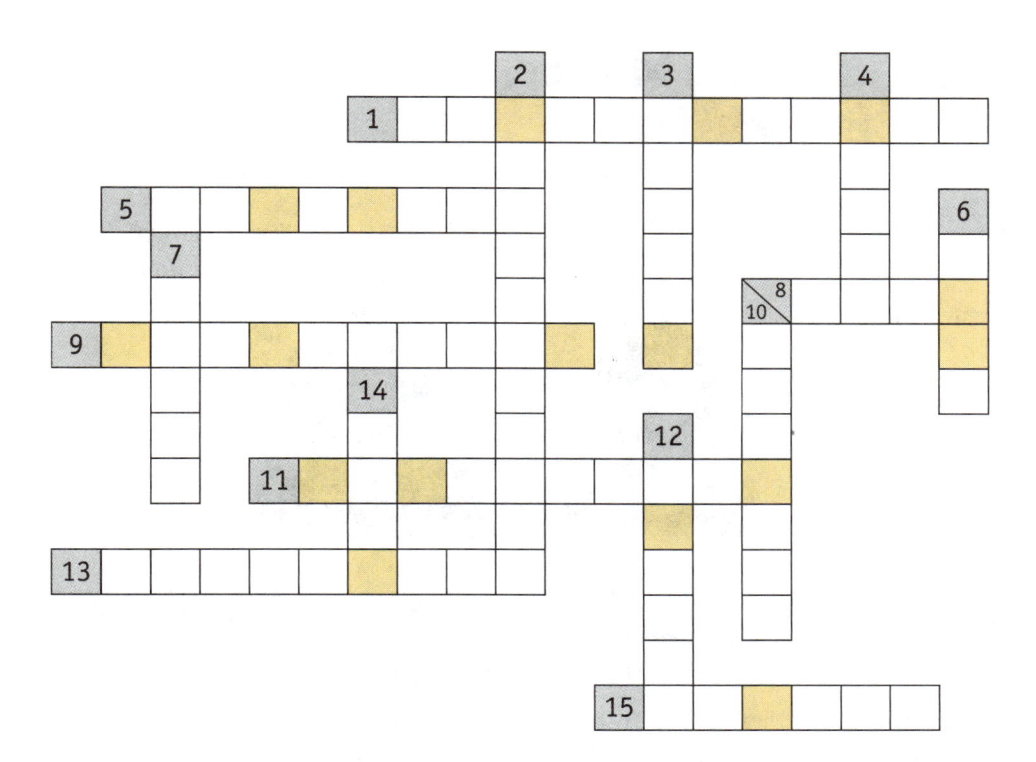

The past is gone and the future isn't here yet, so let's make the
_ _ _ _ _ _ _ _ _ _ _ _ _!

Unit 3 ■ On the Edge

Name: _____ Date: _____ Group: _____

UNIT 4 — Mirror, Mirror…

Modal Auxiliaries

❶ *I think we're lost… We **should** stop and ask someone for directions.*

❷ *Why **would** you listen to a complete stranger? How **could** he possibly know where we're going?*

Focus on…

Modal Auxiliaries

Modal auxiliaries are used with a main verb to change the meaning or tone of a sentence.

They are used to show **capability** and **obligation**, **make requests and deductions**, **give advice** and **grant permission**.

Modal	Function	Example
Can	Capability	• She **can** run very fast.
	Possibility	• She **can** go if she wants to.
Could, would	Offer	• **Would** you like some juice?
	Polite request	• **Could** you help me please?
Should	Advice, suggestion	• You **should** eat more veggies and fewer sweets.
Must, have to	Obligation	• You **must** eat and exercise to stay healthy.
		• You **have to** see a doctor to get a prescription.
May, might	Possibility	• **I may** go to the gym to work out, or **I may** stay home and be a couch potato.
		• She **might** consider breast implants.
		• He **might** grow a moustache.
May, can	Permission	• **May** I go to the gym?
		• **Can** I go, too?
Would	Result of a condition	• If I had more money, I **would** go to Europe.
Could	Possibility	• He **could** be sick.
	Suggestion	• You **could** consider getting contacts.
Must	Deduction	• She **must** think tattoos are cool because she just got her 15th!

Cannot is always written as one word.

⚠️ **PAY ATTENTION!**

Would is also used to express the conditional.
Example: Would you like to have a new hairdo?

Name: _____ Date: _____ Group: _____

Practise!

Use the correct modal to complete the following sentences. The negative form may be used.

a) I ran as fast as possible, but I _____ keep up with him.

b) They _____ be stuck in traffic; otherwise they _____ be here by now.

c) I think that Karen _____ consider consulting a doctor. Her piercing looks gross.

d) If they were less painful, I _____ get a tattoo on my ankle.

e) Your employer _____ not allow tattoos. You _____ check with him first.

f) The operation _____ be performed by a qualified plastic surgeon.

Focus on...

More Possibilities!

Expression or Modal	Function	Example
Would rather	Preference	He **would rather** run than swim.
Had better	Advice	You **had better** get some rest; you look terrible!
Don't have to	No obligation	You **don't have to** see a doctor to buy cough syrup.
Must not	Prohibited action	You **must not** smoke in here.

Practise!

Choose "had better" or "would rather":

a) I _____ call my mom so she doesn't worry.

b) I _____ do 10 pages of English grammar than two math problems.

c) You _____ do your math anyway!

d) He _____ wear his running shoes, but there is so much snow. He _____ wear his boots instead.

e) We _____ be rich and healthy than poor and sick.

ACTIVITY 1

Check your understanding of modals by completing the following text:

A Contest!

_____ you like to vote for your favourite film? You _____ even win $1,000.

You _____ be 18 to vote, but you _____ be a registered member.

You can register online. You _____ vote more than once.

If you are interested, you _____ act now. The contest closes at midnight.

Unit 4 ■ Mirror, Mirror... 73

Name: _____ Date: _____ Group: _____

ACTIVITY 2

The best way to get a feel for using modals is to use them in context.
In this activity, you will create an ad with a job description.

❶ Read the three *Wanted!* ads.

❷ Choose one of them and write an ad of your own.
   a) Describe the qualifications necessary for the job.
   b) Mention at least six qualifications. Use at least four different modals to do this.
   c) Refer to the example for help.
   d) Your text **can** be humorous and you **may** include an illustration!

Wanted!
A dance instructor for a guy with two left feet.

Wanted!
A dog-sitter for a pit bull terrier while owner is in jail.

Wanted!
A door-to-door salesperson to sell beach balls.

Wanted!

• _____
• _____
• _____
• _____
• _____
• _____

Example:

Wanted!
A swimming instructor for very young children.
• You **must** know how to swim.
• You **must not** be allergic to chlorine.
• You **should** be able to remain calm around screaming kids.
• You **may** be asked to change diapers.
• Etc.

74 Unit 4 ■ Mirror, Mirror…   Thank you for not photocopying.   © Éditions Grand Duc

Name: _____ Date: _____ Group: _____

ACTIVITY 3

Now try your hand at this one.

1. **Circle the best auxiliary in each case.**
2. **Be prepared to justify your answers. If necessary, refer to the tables on pp. 72-73.**

Dear Sunny,

I have a friend who is quite a bit overweight. Behind her back, and sometimes even to her face, some of my other friends make fun of her. They are starting to get on my case as well for hanging out with her. I really like Christina a lot, but these guys are my friends, too. They are sure I (would rather/should/have to) be friends with them, but I'm not so sure... What (must/could/should) I do?

Olga

Dear Olga,

Let's look at your friend Christina's weight problem first. You (ought to/could/may) get your friend to see a doctor. Her problem (has to/could/will) be a medical one. If not, there are a few things you (can/have to/must) do. Christina (ought to/might/would) be eating emotionally, especially if she's being chided. Discussing this together (will/has to/may) help. You (don't have to/might/must) also suggest taking an exercise class together. You (would/have to/shouldn't) both benefit and you (might/would/won't) even have fun! Swimming (won't/would/wouldn't) be an excellent choice. In addition, you (would rather/don't have to/could) help your friend make healthy food choices. But, most importantly, whatever you do, you (mustn't/will/don't have to) give up on her.

Peer pressure (doesn't have to/can/would rather) be a difficult issue to deal with. First, you (would rather/have to/must not) try and figure out exactly why your friends are picking on Christina. (Could/May/Should) they be jealous? Perhaps they don't even realize the consequences of their actions. I think that you (don't have to/might not/should) try talking to them about the situation. You (must/shouldn't/couldn't) have to choose between friends, but you (may/will/have to) ask yourself what (can/would rather/doesn't have to) be done to remedy this no-win situation. Listen to your inner voice. You (may/will/have to) know what to do. Good luck!

Sunny Valley

© Éditions Grand Duc   Thank you for not photocopying.   Unit 4 ■ Mirror, Mirror...   **75**

Name: _____ Date: _____ Group: _____

ACTIVITY 4

1 Complete the following statements by adding a question tag.

2 Use the correct form of the modal in the tag ending.

a) That woman should watch what she eats, _____?

b) We don't have to do all of it, _____?

c) They could choose the least expensive option, _____?

d) She has to be at least 14, _____?

e) They would rather train at that gym, _____?

f) They couldn't refuse such a great offer, _____?

ACTIVITY 5

Choose between *may*, *may not*, *must* and *must not*.

a) That woman _____ like tattoos; she has enough of them!

b) The doctors have no choice; they _____ redo the operation.

c) Roger _____ want her to go through with the elective surgery, but ultimately, the choice is hers.

d) She _____ decide not to have breast reduction surgery after all.

e) You _____ be 18 to drink legally, but you _____ get your licence when you are 16.

f) I think she _____ be anorexic. Or perhaps, she's really stressed out.

g) She _____ be out of her mind to keep getting all that cosmetic surgery!

h) He _____ be working out. Look at those biceps!

i) You _____ not like the advice he gives you, but you _____ realize that he's very concerned about your health.

Unit 4 ■ Mirror, Mirror… Thank you for not photocopying. © Éditions Grand Duc

Name: _____ Date: _____ Group: _____

ACTIVITY 6

Choose between *should*, *should not*, *must* and *must not*.

a) You _____ be tired from all that work! How come you're not?

b) He _____ have done an excellent job. Everyone is raving about the results.

c) The sign says that you _____ be at least 16 years old to get a tattoo without parental consent.

d) To compete in that contest, you _____ be between 12 and 15 and attend a public school.

e) Maybe we _____ think about going there in August instead of July.

f) Her family _____ be aware of the situation. It's obvious that there's a serious problem.

g) She _____ speak to Dr. Shank about the problem; I'm sure he could help.

h) He _____ not forget my birthday. After all, it's the same day as his!

i) Write down your PIN and put it in a safe place. It's something you _____ forget!

j) Melina _____ really think twice about getting her tongue pierced. She knows that her parents would not approve and that her boss would fire her.

k) He _____ really have something to be forgiven for. He sent his wife two dozen long-stemmed roses!

l) She _____ learn to drive first. Then she can ask him to lend her his car.

Practise!

Write one sentence using *should* and another one using *must*. Use the statements above to help you, but don't copy them.

a) (should): _____

b) (must): _____

© Éditions Grand Duc — Thank you for not photocopying. — Unit 4 ■ Mirror, Mirror…

Name: _____   Date: _____   Group: _____

ACTIVITY 7

Now choose between shouldn't, doesn't have to and don't have to.

a) You _____ be an expert to participate in the contest.

b) Karen _____ eat so many sweets!

c) Tell William he _____ call first. I'll definitely be home.

d) We _____ write a rough draft this time, but we should take a few minutes to plan our message.

e) If you do decide to get a tattoo, you _____ go to just anyone.

f) Aunt Gemma _____ lift that box; it's too heavy.

g) I really _____ spend that much money on just one item, but I absolutely love that dress!

ACTIVITY 8

This time, choose between might, might not, could and couldn't.

a) Fatima _____ decide which one to buy. She liked them both.

b) Then again, she _____ get either one.

c) It _____ be a good idea to grab a sweater. It's a bit chilly out there.

d) _____ you call them first to see if they still have an opening?

e) The clients might not be 100% satisfied, but they _____ do any better under the circumstances.

f) Wow! I _____ spend hours browsing through their catalogue. There's lots of neat stuff!

Unit 4 ■ Mirror, Mirror…   Thank you for not photocopying.   © Éditions Grand Duc

Name: _____ Date: _____ Group: _____

ACTIVITY 9

Choose the correct modal in parentheses to complete the text. Circle your answers.

Determination

"You (should/must/could) be crazy! You (can't/may not/wouldn't) really expect to make the football team; you're too scrawny! You (should/don't have to/would rather) sign up for something else."

"But I (must/might/can) kick and punt and run!"

"Okay, but (do you have to/can you/will you) tackle?"

He (couldn't/might not/shouldn't). So all summer, Josh worked out. He (would/should/might) show them...

When fall came, he thought he was ready. He knew he still (couldn't/might not/must not) be the biggest guy in school, but he was a lot tougher than before. Unfortunately, once again he didn't make the team. He decided to turn to an ex-player for advice. "You (don't have to/should/will) try these!" the guy told him, showing him a website where you (could/might/have to) buy steroids online. You (don't have to/must/would rather) take them for a long time."

Josh (shouldn't/wouldn't/couldn't) believe his ears! He (would/should/might) never ever use steroids. He knew what they (could/had to/should) do to his health. If that's what it took, he (couldn't/might not/would rather not) be on the team. There (must/would rather/can) be another solution... He thought awhile. "Hey! I (have to/would/might) try out for the soccer team instead. I bet I (should/must/could) make that team!" And he did.

ACTIVITY 10

Complete the following sentences using a modal in your answers.

a) If she really wants her tongue pierced, she... _____

b) He ran out the door before Kim-Lee... _____

c) Believe me! I... _____ than be seen with...

_____

ACTIVITY 11

Choose the correct modals from the Word Bank to fill in the blanks. Cross out each modal you use. There will be one modal left over. Can you find which one? _____

Word Bank

• can	• can	• can't	• could
• don't have to	• don't have to	• had better	• have to
• have to	• may	• might	• might not
• must	• should	• should	• should
• would	• would	• would rather	• wouldn't

Tattoo Turmoil

– Maybe you _____ think about this a bit more... We _____ come back on Saturday.

– Saturday's out. I _____ work. Besides, we're here now. Anyway, why _____ I wait?

– It's expensive... and permanent... and your boss _____ like it.

– My boss! It's none of his business... It's my body.

– True. But, you _____ at least choose a less conspicuous spot. You _____ get one on your temple where everyone _____ see it!

– Where then? On my bum? Or near my navel? Which one _____ you choose? Hey! I just _____ get both! What do you think?

– Frankly, I _____ eat a 100 worms than get a tattoo anywhere. If you want someone to agree with you, you _____ ask Jenna...

– Oh, quit being so straitlaced. You _____ tell me that you _____ like to get a tattoo. Come on! Fess up!

– Not in this lifetime anyway! But, I _____ consider it in the next one...

– Grrr!

– _____ you _____ be 18 anyway? That's what the sign says. Otherwise, you _____ have your parent's consent. Guess you'll _____ wait after all!

– Yeah. Another two years... My mom _____ never give her okay.

– Come on, then! Let's go shopping.

80 Unit 4 ▪ Mirror, Mirror... Thank you for not photocopying. © Éditions Grand Duc

Name: _____ Date: _____ Group: _____

ACTIVITY 12 — Above and Beyond

1. **Read the paragraph below.**
2. **Fill in the missing auxiliaries.**
3. **If you need help, use the Word Bank to the right and refer to the exercises in this unit.**

If...

Oh! If these walls _____ talk, the stories they _____ tell! They _____ certainly share dreams lost in the turbulence of reality and aspirations forgotten on the drawing board. Who knows? They _____ even reveal a secret or two! Something horrible, you really _____ know. An indiscretion that _____ shatter the present... A past event that _____ compromise the future... If these walls _____ talk, all their stories _____ be happy ones so that we _____ sit back and smile and laugh and reminisce together. But, these walls _____ talk, so let's talk to them instead.

Word Bank
- cannot
- could (4)
- might (2)
- shouldn't
- would (3)

ACTIVITY 13 — Above and Beyond

Write a paragraph.

1. **First, complete the sentences below.**
2. **Then, choose one of them and write a paragraph around it.**
3. **Use as many different modal auxiliaries as possible. Highlight them.**

   a) If it really rained cats and dogs, _____
   b) If the moon were made of blue cheese, _____
   c) If mirrors lied, _____

Unit 4 ■ Mirror, Mirror...

Name: _____ Date: _____ Group: _____

The Conditional Tense + an "If-clause"

Focus on...

The Conditional Tense + an "If-clause"

The **conditional tense + an "if-clause"** is used to express a hypothetical or unreal situation.

We say it is hypothetical because it tells us how things would be if the situation were different.

Examples:
  I *would get* breast implants *if I had* enough money. (But I don't have enough money.)
  She *would move* to Japan *if she spoke* Japanese. (But she doesn't speak Japanese.)
  If we wanted to get a tattoo, *we would go* to see Ouzill. (But we don't want to get a tattoo.)

This structure has two parts: – the **main clause** with **the conditional tense**
                                 (would + the base form of the verb)
                                      I *would train*...

                            AND

                                – the **"if-clause"** with **the simple past tense**
                                      if I had...

I would train at least twice a week *if I had* a subscription to the gym.

Exception: In an "if-clause," the verb *to be* takes **were** for all persons:
  If she were any thinner, she would need medical attention.

ACTIVITY 14

Practise using this structure by writing the correct form of the verbs in parentheses and then completing the sentences.

a) If she (to watch) _____ fewer soap operas, _____
_____

b) If she (to be) _____ really on a diet, _____
_____

c) If he (to want, neg.) _____ to go to the game with her, _____
_____

d) If the best things (to come) _____ in small packages, _____
_____

82 Unit 4 ■ Mirror, Mirror...

Name: _____ Date: _____ Group: _____

ACTIVITY 15

Now practise using this structure by putting the words in the right order to make logical sentences.

a) didn't – his – family – have – exist – if – nowhere – shelter – stay – the – to – would

_____
_____

b) if – would – got – her – pierced – she – tongue – kick – her – parents – out – her

_____
_____

c) if – woman – had – any – that – more – would – plastic – she – wear – permanent – surgery – a – mask

_____
_____

d) thinner – she – through – any – soda – would – she – slip – if – the – when – straw – she – a – drank – were

_____
_____

ACTIVITY 16

Complete the following "if-clauses."

❶ **Use both the conditional tense and the modal auxiliary could.**

❷ **Underline the verbs.**

❸ **Use the examples to help you:**

> *Examples:* If I **were** an animal, I**'d be** a bird so I **could fly** to distant lands.
> If she **had** super powers, she **would change** him into a monkey so he **could eat** bananas and **swing** from coconut trees.

a) If I (to be) _____ a musical instrument, _____
_____

b) If money (to grow) _____ on trees, _____
_____

c) If her uncle (to be) _____ a famous rock star, _____
_____

Unit 4 ■ Mirror, Mirror… 83

Name: _____ Date: _____ Group: _____

Here is more practice on using the conditional tense with an "if-clause."

ACTIVITY 17

Practise using this structure by writing the correct form of the verbs in parentheses. Refer to the table on p. 82 if you need help.

a) If you (to run) _____ into her on the street, I don't think you (to recognize) _____ her; she's so thin!

b) He definitely (to know, neg.) _____ how to react if that (to happen) _____ to him.

c) We (to join) _____ an exclusive gym and spa if we (can) _____ afford it.

d) The doctor explained that if she (to undergo) _____ the operation, she (to have to) _____ miss at least three months of school.

e) Daytona thought that if she (to get) _____ his name tattooed on her shoulder, Kirby (to think) _____ that she was cool. Oh, the myths of love!

ACTIVITY 18

Now, fill in the blanks with the correct form of the verbs in parentheses. Then complete the sentences. They must make sense!

a) I _____ if I (to have) _____ the time and the money.

b) She _____ if he (to insist) _____.

c) Shelby said that she _____ if her boyfriend (to get) _____ his nose pierced.

d) Her father (to throw) _____ her out of the house if she _____

e) His friends (to understand, neg.) _____ it if _____

84 Unit 4 ▪ Mirror, Mirror…   Thank you for not photocopying.   © Éditions Grand Duc

Name: _____ Date: _____ Group: _____

UNIT 4 — Wrap-up

ACTIVITY A

① Try to complete the table.
② Check your answers with the tables on pp. 72-73.

MODAL AUXILIARIES		
Modal	**Function**	**Example**
Can	_____ Possibility	She **can** run very fast. She **can** go if she wants to.
_____, **would**	Offer Polite _____	**Would** you like some juice? _____ you help me please?
Should	_____, suggestion	You **should** eat more veggies and fewer sweets.
Must, _____	_____	You **must** eat and exercise to stay healthy. You _____ see a doctor to get a prescription.
_____, **might**	_____	I _____ go to the gym to work out, or I _____ stay home and be a couch potato. She **might** consider breast implants. He **might** grow a moustache.
May, _____	_____	**May** I go to the gym? **Can** I go, too?
Would	Result of a _____	If I had more money, I **would** go to Europe.
Could	_____ _____	He **could** be sick. You **could** consider getting contacts.
_____	Deduction	She _____ think tattoos are cool because she has over 15 on her body.
Note: _____ is also used to express the conditional. _____ you like to have a new hairdo?		

QUICK CHECK

	YES	SOMEWHAT	NO
I was able to fill in all or most of the table correctly.			
I can explain how and when most modals are used.			
What to work on:			

ACTIVITY B

❶ Read the text below.
❷ Circle the correct modal auxiliary.
❸ Be prepared to justify your answers. If necessary, refer to the tables on pp. 72-73.

A "Modal" Husband

While many women (might/should) choose a **model** husband, I (would rather/could) have a **modal** husband. One who (can/would) say, "Honey, (can/should) I get you anything?" And after a long day at work, "Darling, you (can/must) be tired. (Would/May) I pour you a glass of wine before dinner? Maybe we (might/should) go out to eat. Or, we (have to/could) order in. Which (would you rather/could you) do?"

And when it came time for the housework... "Oh, you (cannot/don't have to) do that. You (can/might) strain your back or break a nail. We (can/must) hire a cleaning lady. You (should/might) spend your time having fun or going shopping instead.

Shopping! Yes, my modal husband (would/might) have all the right ideas there as well. "Sweetheart, you really (cannot/ought to) go ahead and buy two outfits, not just one. And you absolutely (may/must) get those sapphire earrings! They do so complement your beautiful eyes. Oh, and while you're at it, you (might/can) as well pick out a designer bag to match those new shoes. I'm sure you (could/must) use a new one! Here, you (can/have to) use my credit card. Yes indeed, the more I think about it, the more I'm going to look for a modal husband. (Can/May) you blame me – for dreaming?

Practise!

List four things a modal wife might do.
Write complete sentences and use... modals!

_____
_____
_____
_____

One Step Further

a) What is a *modal* husband?
_____

b) Why do you think the author chose this term?
_____

Unit 4 ■ Mirror, Mirror...

Name: _____ Date: _____ Group: _____

ACTIVITY C

Complete the puzzle and find the mystery message.

ACROSS

1. You _____ be 18 to vote.
5. Maybe yes, maybe no. They _____ come here in July.
6. Used to give permission: You _____ be seated.
9. It's _____. You must do it!
11. Use "can" to show _____.
13. Use "must" for an _____.
14. I'd _____ do something else.
16. Use "should" when you want to give _____.
18. Either "can" or "may" may be used to give _____.
20. Synonym for "should" (two words) _____

DOWN

2. "Should" is sometimes used to make a _____.
3. "Would" is sometimes used for a _____ situation.
4. If I _____ you, I would get a tattoo!
7. You had _____ consider talking to your parents first. (It would be a good idea.)
8. "Could" and "might" can be used to express _____.
10. Can't is the contraction for _____.
12. Synonym for "must" (two words) _____
15. Use "may" to make a polite _____. May I have your name please?
17. You really _____ think about coming with us. You'd have a great time!
19. It can be a synonym for "will." _____

The mystery message is: ARE YOU __ __ __ __ __ __ __ __ __ ?

Name: _____ Date: _____ Group: _____

UNIT 5 Nothing but the Truth

Adjectives: Comparatives and Superlatives

① Do you think that my story in the newspaper about the fire was **as good as** the one reported on TV?

② No, the story reported on TV was **better than** yours, because the reporter included interviews with eyewitnesses.

③ But the report by the CBC was **the best**, because they had footage of firefighters putting out the blaze.

*Some adjectives use either form.
Examples: quieter, more quiet, simpler, more simple…

*Some adjectives use either "-est" or "most."
Examples: the quietest, the most quiet.

Focus on…

Using Adjectives to Compare Things

Adjectives can be used to make comparisons between two or more things. Adjectives can either be used to show equivalence between two things, compare two things or compare three or more things.

	Equivalent	**Comparative**	**Superlative**
When to use:	Use this structure to "equate" **two** things, or show their "sameness":	Use the **comparative** form to compare **two** things:	Use the **superlative** form to compare **three or more** things:
One-syllable adjectives	as….as as **slow** as	adjective + **er** + than **slower** than	the + adjective + **est** the **slowest**
Two-syllable adjectives ending in: -er, -y, -le	as….as as **scary** as as **brittle** as	(Change **y** to **i**) adjective + **er** + than **scarier** than **brittler** than	(Change **y** to **i**) the + adjective + **est** the **scariest** the **brittlest**
Adjectives with two or more syllables	as …as as **colourful** as as **exciting** as not as **important** as	more/less + adjective + than more **colourful** than more **exciting** than less **important** than	the most/least + adjective the most **colourful** the most **exciting** the least **important**
Irregular comparisons	as **far** as as **many** as as **little** as as **bad** as as **good** as	**farther** than **more** than **less** than **worse** than **better** than	**the farthest** **the most** **the least** **the worst** **the best**

88 Unit 5 ■ Nothing but the Truth   Thank you for not photocopying.   © Éditions Grand Duc

Name: _____ Date: _____ Group: _____

Practise!

1. Complete the following sentences using the comparative form of the adjective provided in parentheses.

a) I like poodles because they are (pretty) _____ beagles.

b) Version 3 of this software program is (advanced) _____ Version 2.

c) Because his house is (far) _____ your house, I would prefer to take the car.

d) While ten apples is (few) _____ twelve apples, eight pears is (many) _____ five pears.

e) Because I did not understand the material from this section of the textbook, I did (bad) _____ my friends on the exam.

f) The new window glass is five times (strong) _____ the original and costs $10 (little) _____ the earlier version. In addition, this new glass is ten times (transparent) _____ the original.

Remember!
Be careful not to mix up **then** – which means next – and **than** – which is used to show comparison.

2. Use the correct form of the comparison for the adjectives in parentheses.

Dreaming

I want to buy a new car, and I am looking at two options – a Ferrari and a Porsche. The Porsche costs (little) _____ the Ferrari and is (good) _____ the Ferrari in terms of fuel economy. The Porsche also seats four people, which is (many) _____ the Ferrari, since it only has two seats. However, Ferrari is (famous) _____ Porsche because the company has won more Formula One trophies. In addition, the engine in the Ferrari is (big) _____ the one in the Porsche, so the Ferrari can go (fast) _____ the Porsche. I am having trouble deciding which car is (practical) _____ the other, but, since I only have $2,000 saved up to buy a car and since both a Porsche and a Ferrari cost (many) _____ $100,000, perhaps I will look into purchasing a good bicycle.

3. Complete the following sentences using the superlative form of the adjective provided in parentheses.

a) This is the (exciting) _____ movie I have seen all year.

b) Health care was the (important) _____ issue in the last election.

c) We went to the (near) _____ grocery store for cookies.

d) They were the (bad) _____ team in the competition.

© Éditions Grand Duc   Thank you for not photocopying.   Unit 5 ■ Nothing but the Truth   89

Name: _____ Date: _____ Group: _____

ACTIVITY 1

1 Write a list of five positive and five negative adjectives that could be used to compare movies.

2 Using those adjectives, write a paragraph comparing two movies that you saw this year.

_____
_____
_____
_____
_____
_____
_____
_____
_____

ACTIVITY 2 Above and Beyond

1 Complete all of the titles below using the superlative of the word in parentheses.

2 Choose one of the titles and write a paragraph on that topic using as many comparative and superlative adjectives as possible.

a) The (Tall) _____ Tree in the World

b) The (Tasty) _____ Dessert in the World

c) The (Good) _____ Cellphone on the Market

d) The Gorilla with the (Long) _____ Arms

_____
_____
_____
_____
_____
_____
_____
_____
_____
_____

Unit 5 ■ Nothing but the Truth   Thank you for not photocopying.   © Éditions Grand Duc

Name: _____ Date: _____ Group: _____

Question Tags

> **Focus on...**
>
> ## Asking and Answering Question Tags
>
> When and how to use question tags:
>
> - Use question tags to confirm information or ask for agreement.
> - With an **affirmative statement**, use a **negative question tag**.
> - With a **negative statement**, use a **positive question tag**.
> - When answering a question tag, you answer the question either in the affirmative or the negative, and then repeat the tag.
>
> The following are examples of how to ask and answer both affirmative and negative question tags:
>
> *Affirmative question:* This speech is exciting, **isn't it**? Answer: Yes, **it is.** **or** No, **it isn't**.
>
> *Negative question:* You don't think it's a lie, **do you**? Answer: Yes, **I do.** **or** No, **I don't**.
>
> *See p. 17 for more details on question tags.*

ACTIVITY 3

Add the correct tag to the following sentences and then answer the questions following the instructions provided in parentheses.

a) This course is interesting, _____? (negative)

_____

b) He didn't finish the race, _____? (positive)

_____

c) She told the truth, _____? (positive)

_____

d) They can't come to the movie, _____? (negative)

_____

e) The dog doesn't have the secret formula, _____? (negative)

_____

f) That bird can't fly, _____? (negative)

_____

g) The car was stolen, _____? (positive)

_____

© Éditions Grand Duc   Thank you for not photocopying.   Unit 5 ■ Nothing but the Truth

Name: _____ Date: _____ Group: _____

Figures of Speech

Focus on...

Figures of Speech

Often associated with literature and poetry, figures of speech involve using words or phrases in order to create images and literary effects. In some cases, as with similes and metaphors, figures of speech are used to create images that can make abstract concepts more concrete – for example, "Love is like a beacon of light shining in the night." In other cases, as with alliteration, figures of speech create literary effects beyond the everyday use of words through their sound or meaning – for example: "Little lions lingered longingly near the carcass."

Most Common Figures of Speech

Figure of Speech	Definition	Examples
1. Metaphor	A comparison between two unlike things or elements.	Susan was a lion in battle.
2. Simile	A comparison – using the words *like* or *as* – between two unlike things or elements.	Susan was like a lion in battle. She is as fast as a cheetah.
3. Personification	Attributing human qualities or abilities to animals or inanimate objects.	The soil thirsts for rain.
4. Irony	A contradiction between what one says and what one means.	As they watched the rain pour down for the sixth straight day, Al turned to Aidan and said, "Nice weather we're having, isn't it?"
5. Hyperbole	The use of exaggerated terms to emphasize a fact or a feeling.	I am so hungry I could eat my right arm.
6. Onomatopoeia	A word that imitates a real sound, such as *crash, bang, pitter patter* or *purring*.	The birds in the park chirped away all morning.
7. Oxymoron	The combination of two terms that are ordinarily contradictory, such as *sweet pain* or *cruel kindness*.	He felt the sting of tough love as he was being spanked by his mother.
8. Alliteration	The repetition of initial consonant sounds.	The red rooster recklessly ran right toward the road.

Name: _____ Date: _____ Group: _____

Practise!

Identify the figures of speech in the following sentences.

a) The engine starts to complain when you go over 140 km/h. _____

b) The moon is like a big pizza in the sky. _____

c) He found himself humming holy hymns high on a hill. _____

d) "Love at 40 Below" is the new single from the icy hot Arctic girl band Frozen Mascara. _____

e) His voice is a warm breeze through my soul. _____

ACTIVITY 4

❶ **Identify whether each sentence contains a simile or a metaphor.**

❷ **Then, explain the comparison between the two elements used in the figure of speech.**

a) My friend is behaving like a lovesick puppy: metaphor or simile

_____
_____
_____

b) Time is but a stream I go a-fishing in. I drink at it: metaphor or simile

_____
_____
_____
_____

c) The journalist conducted the interview like a tiger going straight for the jugular: metaphor or simile

_____
_____

d) Patience is a cat waiting in the grass: metaphor or simile

_____
_____

e) His posture is like a question mark: metaphor or simile

_____
_____

Name: _____ Date: _____ Group: _____

ACTIVITY 5

Rewrite each of the following sentences using either a simile or a metaphor, as indicated at the end of each sentence.

Example: The car is spacious.
1. *As a simile:* The car is like a mansion on wheels.
2. *As a metaphor:* The car is a penthouse on wheels.

a) The exam was extremely difficult. (metaphor)
_____
_____

b) He does not show any emotion. (simile)
_____
_____

c) The bird is singing beautifully. (simile)
_____
_____

d) That song is terrible. (metaphor)
_____
_____

e) She is very tall. (simile)
_____
_____

f) The basement was dark. (metaphor)
_____
_____

Name: _____ Date: _____ Group: _____

ACTIVITY 6 — Above and Beyond

Identify whether each sentence contains a simile or a metaphor and explain the comparison between the two elements used in the figure of speech.

a) Society will unravel like a poorly knitted sweater.

_____
_____
_____

b) The recent economic picture, which seemed hopeful, has faded beyond recognition.

_____
_____
_____

ACTIVITY 7 — Above and Beyond

Underline and identify the figures of speech in the following paragraph.

The New Job

Her new job had become the bane of her existence (_____). She found herself buried under a mountain of work (_____) without any hope of ever again seeing the smiling face of the sun (_____) or shaking the hand of freedom (_____). Her existence was a living death (_____). Then, at 10 p.m., the shrill ringing of her phone jolted her back to the world of the living. It was her best friend Suki offering her a night on the town. Hearing her friend's voice made Toni feel like an inmate on death row receiving a last-minute pardon from the Governor on the way to the electric chair (_____). She was free at last.

The engine of Suki's car hummed (_____) as they drove daringly downtown (_____) to their favourite nightclub. As she began to relax, the music in the bar started to seduce her (_____) and she soon found herself on the dance floor, dancing to disco, jiving to jazz and pounding to punk (_____). She was electricity, her arms flaying and her hips gyrating (_____). But then, she suddenly ran head first into reality – her bullying bombastic boss (_____) was standing right in front of her on the dance floor, eyes trained on Toni and grinning like a cat with a bird in its mouth (_____) as he asked, "Hard at work?" (_____).

© Éditions Grand Duc — Thank you for not photocopying. — Unit 5 ■ Nothing but the Truth

Name: _____ Date: _____ Group: _____

UNIT 5 — Wrap-up

ACTIVITY A

❶ Write a list of 10 adjectives that you would use to describe your favourite type of animal.

❷ Write a paragraph comparing your favourite animal with another animal, using the adjectives from your list.

_____
_____
_____
_____
_____
_____

ACTIVITY B

Complete the following sentences with a simile and then provide an explanation for your comparison.

a) The wet dog smells like _____
_____
_____

b) The sound of the car crash was like _____
_____
_____

c) The boy's face is as red as _____
_____
_____

d) Your painting is like _____
_____
_____

Unit 5 ■ Nothing but the Truth   Thank you for not photocopying.   © Éditions Grand Duc

Name: _____ Date: _____ Group: _____

ACTIVITY C

Complete the crossword puzzle and find the mystery message.

Mystery message:
Unit 5 is the best chapter so far,
_ _ _ _ _ _ _ ?

ACROSS

3. This figure of speech is a comparison of two unlike things or elements. (_____)
4. She has sent you the money, _____?
8. "Tough tasty toffee" is an example of what type of figure of speech? (_____)
11. He has the (many) _____ cavities in the family – nine.
13. A _____ is a comparison of two things or elements that uses "like" or "as."
14. The turtle is (slow) _____ molasses.

DOWN

1. This figure of speech involves attributing human qualities or abilities to animals or inanimate objects. (_____)
2. She flew (far) _____ anyone else in the competition.
5. What type of question is "You find crossword puzzles exciting, don't you?" (_____)
6. Use this type of adjective to compare two things. (_____)
7. Use this form of adjective to compare three or more things. (_____)
9. "Bitter delight" is an example of what type of figure of speech? (_____)
10. He is the (famous) _____ actor in the world.
12. The meat is _____ butter in your mouth.

© Éditions Grand Duc   Thank you for not photocopying.   Unit 5 ■ Nothing but the Truth

UNIT 6 Beyond Reality

Direct and Indirect Speech

① So, let me see if I have this right. According to you, the alien came into your grocery store and **said that he was going to abduct you and take you to Mars.**

② No, that was not what he said. After realizing that he had enough money, the alien actually said, **"Please add the ducks, and I will also take a Mars bar."**

Focus on...

Direct Speech	Indirect Speech (reported speech)
1. Is what someone says word for word.	1. Isn't necessarily word for word.
2. Uses quotation marks.	2. Doesn't use quotation marks.
Example: He said, "Today's movie is about an alien invasion."	Example: He said that today's movie was about an alien invasion.

In the above examples, the verb changes from the **present to the past** because the person who made the original statement said it at some point in the past. As a rule, when using indirect speech to report something that someone said, you go back a tense.

Look at the following chart:

In reported speech, the pronoun often changes. Notice the underlined pronouns in the examples in the table.

Direct Speech	Indirect Speech
Simple present: "*I hate* this movie!" exclaimed Jamal.	**Simple past:** Jamal said that <u>he</u> *hated* that movie.
Present continuous: He said, "*I am reading* a science fiction novel."	**Past continuous:** He said that <u>he</u> *was reading* a science fiction novel.
Present perfect: "*I've lived* with an SF buff for five years," he said.	**Past perfect:** He said that <u>he</u> *had lived* with an SF buff for five years.
Present perfect continuous: "*I've been keeping* this secret for two days," she said.	**Past perfect continuous:** She said that <u>she</u> *had been keeping* the secret for two days.
Simple past: "*I met* the alien last week," said Anna.	**Past perfect:** Anna said that <u>she</u> *had met* the alien last week.
Past continuous: She said, "*We were jogging* earlier."	**Past perfect continuous:** She said that <u>they</u> *had been jogging* earlier.
Past perfect: He said, "The meeting *had* already *started*."	**Past perfect:** NO CHANGE He said that the meeting *had* already *started*.
Past perfect continuous: She said, "*I had* already *been sleeping* for five minutes."	**Past perfect continuous:** NO CHANGE She said that <u>she</u> *had* already *been sleeping* for five minutes.

Name: _____ Date: _____ Group: _____

Practise!

Identify whether the following sentences are examples of direct or indirect speech and circle the correct answer in parentheses.

a) The Galactic Emperor had said that the planet would be destroyed if his demands were not met. (direct/indirect)

b) They say that Charles was the best chess player in the world. (direct/indirect)

c) "Well, there goes the neighbourhood," said the alien when the humanoid moved in next door. (direct/indirect)

ACTIVITY 1

Transform the direct speech in the following sentences to indirect speech.

a) "I am using my time machine every day," he said.
_____

b) "I have been working on this robot all day," said the young boy.
_____

c) She said, "I helped to save the universe last week."
_____

ACTIVITY 2

Transform the indirect speech in the following sentences to direct speech.

a) She said that *Alien* had been her favourite science fiction adventure when she was younger.
_____
_____

b) He said that he was fighting an evil genius who was trying to destroy the world.
_____

c) Sasha said that there had already been an alien in his basement and a spaceship in his backyard by the time he got home.
_____
_____

d) The detective said that she has been chasing the fugitive robot for 10 years.
_____
_____

© Éditions Grand Duc   Thank you for not photocopying.   Unit 6 ▪ Beyond Reality

Active and Passive Voice

① Last night, I **watched** a program about the possibility of life on other planets.

② That program **was watched** by millions of people last night.

③ But very few people watched the news. I **am constantly astonished** at how curious people are about life on other planets and yet how little they **care** about life on Earth.

Focus on...

Active and Passive Voice

In the **active voice**, the **subject** of the sentence **performs the action**.

*Example: Olga **kicked** the ball.*

In the **passive voice**, the **subject** of the sentence **receives the action**. The preposition **by** is often used or implied. The passive voice consists of the verb **to be** followed by a **past participle**.

*Example: The ball **was kicked** by Olga.*

How to form the passive voice:

Subject	Auxiliary	Verb (Past Participle)	Object
Science fiction books	are	written	by aliens.
Science fiction books	were	written	to make people afraid.
Some books	have been	adapted	into movies.

When to use the passive voice:

1. When you want to emphasize the object or give it importance.

Active Voice	Passive Voice
My friend drove the car that hit the cat.	The car that hit the cat **was driven** by my friend.

2. When you do not know the subject.

Active Voice	Passive Voice
X uses publicity stunts to attract customers.	Publicity stunts **are used** to attract customers.

100 • Unit 6 ■ Beyond Reality • Thank you for not photocopying. • © Éditions Grand Duc

Name: _____ Date: _____ Group: _____

Practise!

1. Identify whether these sentences are active or passive.
2. Circle the correct answer in parentheses.
   a) The book was read by everyone in the office. (active/passive)
   b) The pilot flew the plane straight toward the oncoming UFO. (active/passive)
   c) The exams were graded by my guinea pig. (active/passive)

ACTIVITY 3

Change the active voice to the passive voice in the underlined portion of the following sentences.

a) Because *I'm Crazy for You* is their favourite movie, the aliens abducted the actor.
_____
_____

b) I deprogrammed the robot because it was using my credit card to buy clothes on the Internet.
_____
_____

c) The group blew up the factory, and the police arrested them as soon as they tried to escape.
_____
_____

d) They haven't approved your plan to save the universe because they are still having lunch.
_____
_____

ACTIVITY 4

Change the passive voice to the active voice in the following sentences.

a) The news reports about the UFO sighting were seen by millions of people.
_____

b) Before the fire, Tristan had been asked by his roommates to stop playing with matches.
_____

c) He had been taken to Mars in a spaceship by aliens.
_____
_____

d) The dog was taken care of by the neighbours for three weeks.
_____
_____

© Éditions Grand Duc — Thank you for not photocopying. — Unit 6 ■ Beyond Reality

The Past Unreal Conditional

*The birthday party was a disaster. I wish that **I had done** things differently.* ❶

Like what? ❷

*For example, **if I had not rented** the lion for the day, then **I would not have lost** my left arm.* ❸

Focus on...

The Past Unreal Conditional

The **past unreal conditional** is used to speak about **imaginary situations in the past**.

- Use it to describe:
  - What you would have done differently
  - How something might have happened differently if circumstances had been different
- Use the following form:

  [**If + past perfect**..., ... **would have + past participle**...]

Example: **If they had not invented** the car, society **would have evolved** in a different way.

Practise!

Complete the sentence in the past unreal conditional using the correct form of the verb in parentheses.

a) If my sister (join) _____ the army, then I (move) _____ out of the tool shed and into her room.

b) Aliens (contact) _____ us years ago if we (stop) _____ polluting the atmosphere.

c) If scientists (invent) _____ not _____ gunpowder, then we (discover) _____ other ways to kill one another.

Unit 6 ■ Beyond Reality

Name: _____ Date: _____ Group: _____

ACTIVITY 5

Complete the sentences using the correct form of the past unreal conditional.

a) The gorilla would have helped the little boy if the boy _____
_____

b) If the kite had not got stuck in the tree, the father _____
_____

c) The car would not have hit the tree if the driver _____
_____

d) If the pilot would have listened to the air traffic controller, the plane _____
_____
_____

e) If the boxer had eaten breakfast, then he _____
_____
_____

f) I would have done better on the exam if I _____
_____
_____

ACTIVITY 6

❶ **In the space provided below, write a one-paragraph answer to one of the following questions.**

❷ **Use the past unreal conditional as often as possible in your answer.**

   a) If aliens had been discovered living on the moon, how would life on Earth have changed?

   OR

   b) If scientists had built a robot that was actually alive, how would life have changed?

_____
_____
_____
_____
_____

Unit 6 ▪ Beyond Reality

Name: _____ Date: _____ Group: _____

ACTIVITY 7

In the space provided below, use the past unreal conditional to imagine what circumstances would have helped you to fulfill your wish. Structure your answer as an "if-clause."

Example: I wish I had passed my driving test.
What circumstances would have fulfilled your wish? <u>I would have passed my driving test</u> if <u>I had remembered that coffee upsets my stomach.</u>

a) I wish I had finished my presentation.

What circumstances would have fulfilled your wish? _____
_____
_____

b) I wish I had gone to visit her in the hospital.

What circumstances would have fulfilled your wish? _____
_____
_____

c) I wish I had called you earlier.

What circumstances would have fulfilled your wish? _____
_____
_____

d) I wish I had graduated from university.

What circumstances would have fulfilled your wish? _____
_____
_____

e) I wish I had gone on the spaceship.

What circumstances would have fulfilled your wish? _____
_____
_____

Unit 6 ■ Beyond Reality

Name: _____ Date: _____ Group: _____

ACTIVITY 8

1 Choose one of the following scenarios and write a paragraph explaining what you think would have happened if...

2 Use the past unreal conditional as often as possible in your answer.

a) What would have happened if you had woken up this morning to discover that you were a giant beetle?

OR

b) What would have happened if you had been abducted by aliens last night?

OR

c) What would have happened if scientists had discovered that dogs could speak?

OR

d) What would have happened if you had discovered last week that your best friend was a robot?

_____
_____
_____
_____
_____
_____
_____
_____
_____
_____
_____
_____
_____
_____
_____
_____
_____
_____
_____
_____

Name: _____ Date: _____ Group: _____

Confusables – Homonyms and Vocabulary Building

① *I couldn't believe it! Juan came over yesterday for the surprise birthday party, and he **ate** the **whole** cake.*

② *He came over and had **eight hole** cakes? What is the main ingredient in **hole** cakes?*

> Refer to p. 278 in the Toolkit of your Student Book for a list of words that are difficult to spell.

Focus on…

Homonyms and Vocabulary Building

Spelling words properly in English can be quite difficult. There are many rules to keep in mind, but there are also many exceptions. While you could learn them by heart, it is just as effective to use a dictionary.

Among the most confusing aspects of learning to read and write in English are **homonyms** – words that sound alike but are usually spelled differently and have different meanings. For example, although they sound the same, *whether* is used to refer to alternative possibilities, as in "whether he comes or stays home," and *weather* means the atmospheric conditions outside, as in "the weather was wet and rainy."

Practise!

1. Circle the correct homonym in the parentheses to complete the sentence.

a) (They're/Their/There) spaceship is still in the docking bay, so I think (they're/their/there) still on board the space station.

b) There is a good chance you will (loose/lose) your watch because it is too (loose/lose).

c) I am not sure (whether/weather) we should go to the game; it will depend on the (whether/weather).

106 Unit 6 ■ Beyond Reality   Thank you for not photocopying.   © Éditions Grand Duc

2. **Complete the sentence by circling the correct spelling for the word given in parentheses.**

   a) His (ommision/**omission**/omision) cost him his freedom.

   b) *Ship* and *slip* is an example of two words that (ryme/rhym/**rhyme**).

   c) Their message for help was heard (accros/ackros/**across**) the galaxy.

   d) According to the new intergalactic (**calendar**/calender/calander), April 16 is Faflovian Independence Day on Sigma 5.

   e) Knights like Sir Lancelot lived in (medievil/**medieval**/midevil) times.

   f) To (**possess**/posess/posses) a gun without a licence is illegal, but you do not need a permit to own a pair of (sissors/scisors/**scissors**).

ACTIVITY 9

Circle the correct word in parentheses to complete the sentences in this story.

You Want to Win the Lottery, Don't You?

Despite the bad (**weather**/whether), Thea and Pardeep, (who's/**whose**) brother worked on the special (**effects**/affects) for the latest science fiction movie, walked to the store to buy an "Instant (**Millionaire**/Milionaire/Milionnaire)" lottery ticket. The next day, they discovered that they had bought the winning ticket! When they told (there/**their**/they're) (freind/fiend/**friend**) Alma, she said, "But (**who's**/whose) the (**millionaire**/milionaire/milionnaire)? (**Who's**/Whose) ticket is it?" Thea said, "(Its/**It's**) mine, of course."

Not surprisingly, Pardeep did not agree. "No, (its/**it's**) mine."

(**Through**/Threw) the (**night**/nite/nigth), the (to/**two**/too) girls flung insults at one another. (Than/**Then**) the next morning, Alma came over and told them that, because of a computer malfunction, the winning tickets were no longer valid and a new draw would be held next (weak/**week**). To this day, (nether/**neither**/niether) friend has ever apologized for (there/**their**/they're) behaviour, and I do not feel that it is my place to offer them any (advise/**advice**).

Name: _____ Date: _____ Group: _____

UNIT 6 — Wrap-up

ACTIVITY A

❶ Choose the correct spelling of the word in parentheses and then rewrite the sentence in the passive voice.

❷ Use the original sentence to write a sentence in the past unreal conditional.

> *Example:* Active voice: John kicked the (ball/bale).
> Passive voice: The ball **was kicked** by John.
> Past unreal conditional: **If John had kicked** the ball, then the World Cup **would have been** ours.

a) Joshua is flying the spaceship (allot/a lot/alot).

Passive voice: _____

Past unreal conditional: _____

_____

_____

b) Her (vehicle/veacle/vehical) caused the (traffic/trafick/traffic) jam.

Passive voice: _____

Past unreal conditional: _____

_____

_____

c) The parents (allowed/aloud) their dog to use the computer and send emails to his friends.

Passive voice: _____

Past unreal conditional: _____

_____

_____

_____

_____

Unit 6 ■ Beyond Reality   Thank you for not photocopying.   © Éditions Grand Duc

Name: _____ Date: _____ Group: _____

ACTIVITY B

Complete the crossword puzzle and solve the mystery message.

Mystery Message:

The __ __ __ __ __ __ are coming!

ACROSS

1. _____ is not necessarily word for word and does not use quotation marks.
5. Which word refers to location: wear, were or where?
8. If you had read the chapter carefully, you would have recognized this sentence as being in the _____ conditional.
9. "The crossword was completed by me" uses the _____ voice.
10. If I had known that this puzzle was too easy, I _____ included harder clues.
11. "The Mars probe sent back images of the planet's surface" uses the _____ voice.

DOWN

2. A sentence that records what someone says word for word.
3. He said that his dog _____ sleeping for six hours.
4. Can you (reed/read) this clue?
6. The words "see" and "sea" are _____.
7. Choose the correct spelling of this word – ezagerate or exaggerate or exagerate?

Unit 6 ■ Beyond Reality

Name: _____ Date: _____ Group: _____

UNIT 7 — Wondering About Wonders

Placement of Adjectives

① When did you get back from Peru?

② Last week. It was really fantastic. We visited the **most beautiful old Inca** settlement.

③ What else did you see?

④ We also saw an Inca temple. It was built using **enormous irregular-shaped old** stones.

⑤ One day, I'd like to visit one of these **magnificent ancient South American** civilizations.

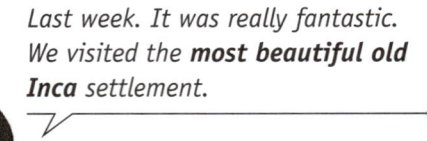

Focus on...

Placement of Adjectives

Notice that commas do not always separate the adjectives.

In English, **adjectives** almost always go **before** the **nouns** they describe:

Examples: **seven** wonders, a **round** coliseum, an **ancient** ruin...

Sometimes, we want to describe a noun with more than one adjective. The general order is:

Opinion	before	Fact
An opinion is what you **think** about the noun.		A fact is what is **definitely true** about the noun.
Example: a **wonderful** monument		Example: a **natural** wonder

Determiner or Number	Opinion	Size	Shape	Age	Colour	Origin	Material	Qualifier	Noun
A	beautiful	big	round		white	Italian	marble	dining	table
Four	marvellous	huge		old		Greek		Doric	columns

Note

Sometimes this order is changed to show emphasis.

Example: A beautiful big round **Italian** white marble dining table.

Practise!

1. Use at least three adjectives to describe the following nouns.

a) car _____

b) movie _____

c) type of food _____

d) television show _____

110 Unit 7 ■ Wondering About Wonders

Name: _____ Date: _____ Group: _____

2. Put the following adjectives in the correct order. Be ready to justify your answer.

a) [a – beautiful – brass – enormous] statue
_____

b) [a – English – fabulous – round – stone] monument
_____

c) [a – blue – breathtaking – crystal – Italian – old] vase
_____

d) [an – expensive – French – tall – old – wine] bottle
_____

e) [a – antique – gorgeous – little – Peruvian – silver] hatpin
_____

ACTIVITY 1

Put the adjectives in parentheses in the correct order.

Quebec's Contribution to UNESCO's World Heritage

Canada has 14 sites on UNESCO's World Heritage list, two of which are in Quebec. The first is Miguasha National Park and the second is Old Quebec. As you tour Old Quebec, you realize why it is considered a World Heritage site. Place Royale, (a – grey – small – square – stone) _____ plaza, and the Promenade des Gouverneurs, (a – wooden – long – big) _____ terrace overlooking the St. Lawrence River, are two of the many attractions worth visiting. At the end of this terrace is (a – steep – wooden – long) _____ staircase leading to the Citadelle on the Plains of Abraham. The Chateau Frontenac is also situated on the Promenade des Gouverneurs. This (brown – old – big – brick) _____ monument towers over the Promenade. The entrance to the hotel is paved with (square – enormous – grey) _____ stones dating from a century or more ago. Many streets also deserve to be seen. La Rue du Trésor, (a – European-style – short – narrow) _____ street is alive with artists selling their paintings. Quebec truly deserves to be on UNESCO's list.

© Éditions Grand Duc   Thank you for not photocopying.   Unit 7 ■ Wondering About Wonders   111

Gerunds and Infinitives

❶ What other great wonder are you going to visit?

❸ Really! I thought you disliked **travelling** long hours on a plane.

❷ My girlfriend always dreamed about **seeing** the Iguazu Falls in Argentina.

❹ I know, but she really wants **to see** the falls. And what she wants, she gets.

> **Focus on...**

Gerunds and Infinitives

Gerunds and infinitives are forms of verbs that act as nouns.

A. A **gerund** is a noun formed by adding **-ing** to a verb. *Example: play/**playing***

A gerund can be the **subject** of a sentence. *Example:* **Visiting** *historical sites is his pastime.*	A gerund can be the **object** of a sentence. *Example: He enjoys* **visiting** *old buildings.*

The **negative form** of a gerund is made by adding **not** before the gerund.
Example: He really prefers **not working** *if he has a choice.*

B. Infinitives are the "to" form of verbs. *Example: play/**to play***

An infinitive can be the **subject** of a sentence. *Example:* **To speak** *English is useful.*	An infinitive can be the **object** of a sentence. *Example: They want* **to speak** *Spanish.*

The **negative form** of an infinitive is made by adding **not** before the infinitive.
Example: He prefers **not to travel** *alone.*

The following verbs are **always followed by a gerund**:	The following verbs are **always followed by an infinitive**:
admit, advise, appreciate, avoid, can't help, complete, consider, delay, deny, detest, dislike, <u>enjoy</u>, escape, excuse, finish, forbid, get through, imagine, mind, miss, permit, postpone, practise, quit, recall, report, resent, resist, resume, risk, spend (time), suggest, tolerate, waste (time). *Example: We <u>enjoy</u> **learning** about strange places.*	agree, aim, appear, arrange, ask, attempt, be able, beg, begin, build, care, choose, consent, continue, dare, decide, deserve, detest, dislike, expect, fail, <u>forget</u>, get, happen, have, hesitate, hope, hurry, intend, leap, leave, like, love, mean, neglect, offer, plan, prefer, prepare, promise, refuse, remember, say, shoot, start, stop, swear, try, use, wait, want, wish. *Example: She <u>forgot</u> **to validate** her passport.*

The following verbs can be followed by either **a gerund or an infinitive** with little difference in meaning:
cease, continue, hate, like, love, neglect, <u>prefer</u>, propose.
Example: He <u>prefers</u> **to read** *about a country. He <u>prefers</u>* **reading** *about a country.*

ACTIVITY 2

Highlight or underline the appropriate word in parentheses to complete the sentences.

a) A fire was kept (to burn/burning) at the top of the lighthouse of Alexandria.

b) The fire was intended (to guide/guiding) ships in from the sea.

c) The word mausoleum came (to mean/meaning) a large tomb.

d) The statue of Zeus at Olympia was built (to honour/honouring) the king of the gods.

e) Over 2 million blocks were used (to erect/erecting) the Great Pyramid.

f) The Hanging Gardens of Babylon were designed by a king who hoped (to please/pleasing) his wife.

g) It took 12 years (to build/building) the Colossus of Rhodes.

h) An arsonist eventually succeeded in (to burn/burning) down the Temple of Artemis.

i) The ancient Egyptians believed in (to preserve/preserving) the bodies of their dead pharaohs intact inside pyramids.

j) The Colossus of Rhodes was completed (to use/using) the metal of the weapons left behind when an enemy force failed (to take/taking) the island.

k) The statue of Zeus was moved from its original place by people who hoped (to preserve/preserving) it intact.

l) The pyramids of Egypt are the only examples of the Seven Wonders of the Ancient World that we continue (to marvel/marvelling) at today.

m) Slaves constantly turned huge wheels (to irrigate/irrigating) the Hanging Gardens.

n) Can you imagine (to contemplate/contemplating) all of the Seven Wonders today?

o) After the Temple of Artemis burned down, women offered (to sell/selling) their jewels to raise money to rebuild it.

Name: _____ Date: _____ Group: _____

ACTIVITY 3   Above and Beyond

1 Read the following sentences. Put a check mark (✔) if the sentence is correct or a cross (✘) if the sentence is incorrect.

a) The pyramids at Chichen Itza in Mexico are beautiful old big structures. (   )

b) We plan to visit them in the near future. (   )

c) Christ the Redeemer in Rio de Janeiro, Brazil, is a breathtaking tall white statue of Christ. (   )

d) It appears protecting the city of Rio de Janeiro. (   )

e) The Roman Coliseum is an old round beautiful ruin. (   )

f) Upon seeing it, you refuse to imagine the cruelty that took place there. (   )

g) The Great Wall of China is a long brown stone structure that can be seen from space. (   )

h) At least that is what we were taught to believing. (   )

i) Machu Picchu, perched high in the luxuriant green tall mountains of Peru, is still shrouded in mystery. (   )

j) Caretakers of Machu Picchu disapprove of anyone straying from the regular paths. (   )

k) Petra, with its awe-inspiring tall pink stone columns, is a sight to be seen. (   )

l) I'm sure you recall seeing it at the end of an Indiana Jones movie. (   )

m) The Taj Mahal, a white enormous mausoleum, is a true poem to love. (   )

n) When you see it for the first time, you can't help wondering about what true love really is. (   )

o) The Colossus of Rhodes was a tall beautiful copper statue. (   )

p) People would spend hours to contemplate its magnificence. (   )

q) Today, people just happen to react in the same way in front of the Statue of Liberty. (   )

r) They refuse admitting that it is simply a lifeless object made of steel. (   )

s) It is simply a tall green metal representation of a woman. (   )

t) The Colossus was only a copper tall representation of a man. (   )

2 Choose five of the incorrect sentences from above and correct them.

a) _____

b) _____

c) _____

d) _____

e) _____

Unit 7 ■ Wondering About Wonders

3 Write a gerund or an infinitive to complete the following sentences.

To Cheat or not to Cheat

Jack was an archaeology student at a very famous university. His parents were proud of him and would tell anyone and everyone (listen) _____ all the exploits that their darling boy had done during the semester. Jack was a rather lazy person who really disliked (study) _____. He would rather avoid (work) _____ altogether if he could. His mid-term exam was coming up very soon and he had (study) _____ very hard if he wanted (succeed) _____. He intended (pass) _____ the exam as best as he could, but he postponed (study) _____ until the very last minute. He tried (read) _____ all he could on the subject the night before the exam, but it was really too much. He challenged himself (read) _____ at least half the material. It was no use. He considered (be) _____ sick on the day of the exam, but it would only delay the inevitable and his professor would not accept that excuse. Finally, he decided (cheat) _____. He wrote all that he could on his arms and wore a long-sleeved shirt to the exam.

All went well? You would think so, wouldn't you? He tried (convince) _____ himself that it was for the best and that his parents would continue (be) _____ proud of him. Unfortunately, Jack forgot that the answers were still on his arms when he rolled up his sleeves before leaving the classroom. He tried (explain) _____ to his professor that they were only tattoos. It didn't work. He finally admitted to (cheat) _____ on the test and promised never (do) _____ it again if he were given another chance. Out of great sympathy, or so he thought, his professor permitted him (take) _____ the test over. Jack was so happy, he offered (buy) _____ the professor lunch. His professor thanked him but refused (share) _____ a lunch with Jack. Then he told Jack that plagiarism was a serious offence and to discourage him from (cheat) _____ again, he could take the test over but only at the end of next semester. He told Jack not to worry about (study) _____ this time, the questions would probably be the same and he should have no problem with them. He also warned him (wash) _____ his arms before coming to class next semester.

Phrasal Verbs

① *Do you **feel up to** looking at some pictures from my last trip?*

③ *Come on, just a few pictures.*

⑤ *As long as you **don't pass out**.*

② *I don't want to **let you down**, but I'm really tired.*

④ *Okay, but you won't **get ticked off** if I **nod off**, will you?*

Focus on...

Phrasal Verbs

A **phrasal verb** is composed of a **verb** and a **particle** (a preposition).

Adding this preposition to the verb gives a new meaning to the original verb.

Examples: To **look**: to use the eyes to see.
To **look after**: to take care of someone, something.
To **break**: to make something come apart in pieces; smash, crack or split.
To **break up**: to end a relationship.

Here is a list of common phrasal verbs. Refer to pp. 128 and 129 of the Reference Section for more phrasal verbs.

Phrasal Verb	Meaning
to bone up on	to review/to study thoroughly for a short time
to catch on (to)	to develop understanding or knowledge of something
to chicken out	to lose the courage or confidence to do something
to clam up	to suddenly become quiet/to refuse to talk about something
to come down with	to become sick
to count on	to depend on
to feel up to	to feel strong enough or comfortable enough to do something
to fill in for	to temporarily do someone else's work/to substitute for another person
to hold up	to delay
to keep on	to continue
to knock oneself out	to do something with more zeal than what is expected
to let down	to disappoint
to look forward to	to anticipate pleasantly/to think about a pleasant thing before it happens
to look into	to investigate/to get more details about something
to nod off	to fall sleep
to pass out	to faint/to lose consciousness
to pitch in	to help/to join together to accomplish something
to stand out	to be noticeably better than other similar people or things
to show up	to arrive/to appear
to wrap up	to finish something/to bring something to a conclusion

Unit 7 ■ Wondering About Wonders   Thank you for not photocopying.   © Éditions Grand Duc

Name: _____ Date: _____ Group: _____

ACTIVITY 4

Rewrite the following sentences using the appropriate phrasal verb. Don't forget to put the verbs in the correct tense.

a) The exam was just around the corner, so they decided to <u>study</u> the subject <u>thoroughly</u>.
_____

b) Since Jack was away on sick leave, I decided to <u>replace him temporarily</u>.
_____

c) She did not want to <u>disappoint</u> her father, so she went to medical school.
_____

d) Everybody <u>joined together</u> and rebuilt the garage that had burned down.
_____

e) The traffic was <u>delayed</u> because of the demonstration.
_____

f) When asked about the incident, he <u>suddenly refused to talk</u>.
_____

g) He finally <u>arrived</u> one hour late.
_____

h) During the conference, he kept <u>falling asleep</u>.
_____

i) After two hours, they finally <u>understood</u> how the computer worked.
_____

j) This last number <u>finishes</u> this exercise.
_____

ACTIVITY 5

Write five sentences of your own using phrasal verbs from the list above or from the Reference Section.

a) _____
b) _____
c) _____
d) _____
e) _____

Idiomatic Expressions

① How were the pyramids?

② Fantastic. **Nothing can hold a candle** to them.

③ Really. Let me be **the devil's advocate** for a moment. Are they better that the Mayan temples you saw last year?

④ Not the same thing at all. You should visit them before you **kick the bucket**.

Focus on...

Idiomatic Expressions

Idiomatic expressions or idioms are expressions, often linked to an image, which are used to express something figuratively. Here are a few common idiomatic expressions. Refer to p. 130 of the Reference Section for more idioms.

Idiom	Meaning
to be as clean as a whistle	not involved in anything illegal
as good as new	kept as when it was new, or repaired as good as it was new
a (whole) new ball game	a completely different situation
a new broom	a new leader who makes a lot of changes and improvements
ace in the hole	a secret weapon or a sure thing
to be new to the game	to lack any experience of a particular activity
to break new ground	to do something that is different to anything that has been done before
can't hold a candle to	they are not at all comparable in quality
a dead ringer	a person who bears a close resemblance to someone else
to play devil's advocate	a person who espouses a cause just for the sake of argument
to give someone a new lease on life	new energy after a period of illness or sadness
in a New York minute	very quickly
mad as a hatter	refers to any crazy person or someone who acts crazy
new blood	new people in an organization who will provide new ideas and energy
That's a new one on me.	surprising fact or idea that you have never heard before
the new kid on the block	someone who is new in a place or organization
to kick the bucket	to die
to turn over a new leaf	to start behaving in a different way
under the weather	to be sick
You can't teach an old dog new tricks.	difficult to make someone change the way they do something when they have been doing it the same way for a long time

Name: _____ Date: _____ Group: _____

ACTIVITY 6

Write the idiom that corresponds to the illustration.

Answer: _____

Answer: _____

Answer: _____

Answer: _____

Answer: _____

Answer: _____

ACTIVITY 7

The idioms in the following sentences have been mixed up. Rewrite these sentences by replacing the incorrect idioms with the correct ones.

a) My friend just started working here; one could say he is <u>as clean as a whistle</u>.

_____

b) After that close brush with death, George decided <u>he was a dead ringer</u>.

_____

c) No one can <u>turn over a new leaf</u> to Hank. He's truly the best in the sport.

_____

d) I was sure I met the Prime Minister. That guy <u>can hold a candle</u>.

_____

e) The Customs agents checked his credentials. He's <u>new to the game</u>.

_____

Name: _____ Date: _____ Group: _____

UNIT 7 — Wrap-up

ACTIVITY A

Rewrite the following sentences using the appropriate idiomatic expression.

Example: My grandfather said it was too late for him to <u>learn something new</u>.
My grandfather said you **can't teach an old dog new tricks**.

a) That trip to Egypt gave Dave the <u>energy</u> he needed after his breakup with Suzy.
_____

b) The two weeks in Peru went by <u>extremely fast</u>.
_____

c) Even though they tried to blame him for the incident, he came out of it <u>spotless</u>.
_____

d) When he wants to, my friend Jacques can be <u>very, very crazy</u>.
_____

e) After his accident, Henry came out of the hospital <u>without any complications</u>.
_____

f) When I last saw Kathy' she seemed a bit <u>sick</u>.
_____

g) That girl <u>looks just like</u> Marilyn Monroe.
_____

h) My vote goes to her. She will <u>be a great leader and turn things around</u>.
_____

i) She is continuously <u>arguing</u> no matter what we say.
_____

j) <u>Things have changed</u>. Now we might have a word to say in the situation.
_____

Name: _____ Date: _____ Group: _____

ACTIVITY B

❶ Read the sentences below.

❷ Choose phrasal verbs or idioms from the Word Bank to complete the sentences.

Word Bank

- a new one on me
- kicked the bucket
- play devil's advocate
- looking forward to
- knock yourself out
- keep on
- pitch in
- chicken out
- count on
- pass out
- can't hold a candle to
- under the weather
- whole new ball game
- came down with
- new to the game
- show up
- feels up to
- as good as new
- hold up
- stood out
- looked into

a) That's _____. I never realized what a history buff you were.

b) Well, if you like reading so much, here's the key to the library. Go on, have fun, _____.

c) I'm _____ visiting one of the New Seven Wonders of the World.

d) No matter how marvellous they are, they _____ the original Seven Wonders of the World.

e) Some people _____ when they see something as beautiful as Petra. It is known as the Stendhal Syndrome.

f) We decided to take the Inca Trail to Machu Picchu. Your friend may join us if he _____ it.

g) He says he'll follow us along the Inca Trail, but I'm sure he'll _____ as he always does.

h) If he doesn't come, it's not because he's afraid; it's because he's feeling a bit _____.

i) I'm sure you're right about all that, but let me _____ for a minute.

j) Gee, I never saw it like that. If what you're saying is true, then it's a _____.

k) Do you think we can _____ him to follow us up the trail all the way to Machu Picchu?

l) Yes, I'm sure he won't _____ the group. He'll _____ walking no matter what.

m) What about his history of health problems? You know, I _____ his medical records.

n) He's _____. Don't worry he'll _____ and he'll _____ to make this trek memorable.

o) I hope so. Remember, he's _____ and it can be difficult the first time.

p) He can do it. Last year he walked the whole Great Wall of China and really _____ among the group.

q) I know, but remember when we visited the statue of Christ the Redeemer in Rio, he's the only one who _____ a cold.

r) Maybe, but at least he hasn't _____.

© Éditions Grand Duc   Thank you for not photocopying.   Unit 7 ▪ Wondering About Wonders   121

Name: _____ Date: _____ Group: _____

ACTIVITY C

Complete the crossword puzzle and find the mystery message.

ACROSS

2. Christ the Redeemer in _____ is an **impressive tall white statue** overlooking the city.
4. My father was very angry. Boy, did he ever _____ me out.
5. The **mad hatter** was the _____ character in Alice in Wonderland.
10. A friend of mine once qualified the _____ as **a big old brown pile** of stones.
12. One of the New Seven Wonders of the World located in Peru.
15. If something is not an opinion, it is probably a _____.
18. He **faced up** to the facts and admitted his _____ in the matter.
19. Many people have **looked into** the mystical meaning of the number _____
20. This city is quoted in an idiom meaning very quickly.
21. In a string of adjectives, _____ goes before age.
22. Some people like playing **devil's advocate** just for the sake of _____.

DOWN

1. No modern _____ **can hold a candle to** the Taj Mahal.
3. When you reach an agreement with someone, it could be said you _____ your problems.
4. The Colossus of Rhodes was **a beautiful tall** _____ statue.
6. What you can't teach an old dog.
7. When you are much, much better than all the others, it is said you _____.
8. An idiom expresses something _____.
9. A preposition gives a new _____ to a verb.
11. Someone who **digs up** clues about lost civilizations is an _____.
13. What you say about someone that looks very much like someone else.
14. _____ **read up on** and study what archaeologists have uncovered.
16. A noun formed by adding **-ing** to a verb.
17. The material that **stood out** on the Colossus of Rhodes was _____.

122 Unit 7 ■ Wondering About Wonders

Name: _____ Date: _____ Group: _____

Mystery sentence: _ _ _ _   _ _ _   _ _ _ _ _ _ _ .

Name: _____ Date: _____ Group: _____

REFERENCE SECTION A

Capitalization

In English, capital letters are used in the following ways:

1.	**The first word in a sentence** *T*he cat is on the table.
2.	**The pronoun "I"** I said that *I* would call him after school.
3.	**The names of…** • **People:** Terry Fox, Nelson Mandela, Meagan Winslow • **Relatives when used with the person's name:** *U*ncle Tom, *A*unt Agatha • **Titles when they are included with the person's name:** *D*etective Brady, *M*ajor Lucie Madison, *M*s. Jeannette Turner, *D*r. Albert • **Places:** Nova Scotia, Lake Louise, Harvard, New York City, the Eiffel Tower • **Planets, stars and constellations:** Uranus, Earth, Venus, the Big Dipper • **Events:** the Miss Universe Contest, the Quebec Winter Carnival, the Stanley Cup • **Days and months:** Tuesday, Thursday, February • **Holidays and holy days:** Christmas, Kwanzaa, Valentine's Day, Yom Kippur • **Languages, nationalities, races and religions:** English, Chinese, Europeans, African-American, Jewish, Buddhism • **Organizations:** the United Nations, the Salvation Army • **Organizations that use acronyms (all capitals):** UN (*U*nited *N*ations), NHL (*N*ational *H*ockey *L*eague) • **Brands or trademarks:** Jell-O, Kleenex
4.	**Lists, when the elements are on separate lines:** like the above list
5.	**The first word in a direct quotation:** He said, "*C*all me tomorrow."
6.	**Only the first word in the closing of a letter:** *Y*ours truly, *V*ery sincerely, *W*ith love, *Y*our friend

124 Reference Section A   Thank you for not photocopying.   © Éditions Grand Duc

ACTIVITY 1

Rewrite the following sentences and use the appropriate capital letters.

a) we finally got to see the movie *titanic* after all these years.
___

b) my english-speaking peruvian friend was of great help during that trip.
___

c) we left on monday, june 2 and returned on friday, august 6. when we arrived in peru, it was wintertime.
___

d) a few weeks after the prime minister's visit, the secretary-general of the united nations dropped by to say hello.
___
___

d) there is a box of kleenex on my teacher's desk.
___

ACTIVITY 2

Underline the letters that should be capitalized in the following texts.

dear doctor herbert,

last christmas, my wife cynthia fell sick. i was told by aunt hortensia that if i gave her a bag of kool-aid powder every hour, she would get better. it doesn't work. by new year's day, not only was she not feeling better, but there was a constant dusting of kool-aid everywhere. she keeps complaining that she is thirsty and with all the powder she has swallowed so far, i'm afraid of what will happen if i give her water.

please help!

very sincerely,

john

dear john, you nitwit,

take cynthia to the hospital right away and tell aunt hortensia to stop practising medicine without a license or i will report her to the ramq.

sincerely,

dr. hubert herbert, md

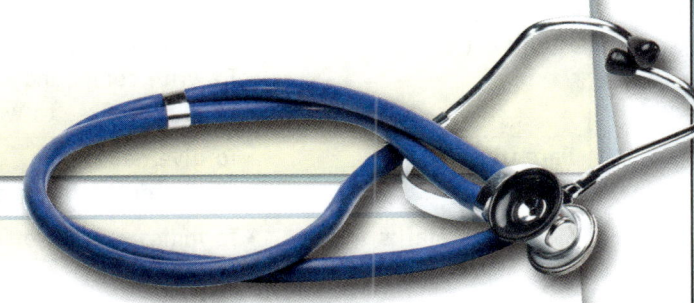

Name: _____ Date: _____ Group: _____

REFERENCE SECTION B

Punctuation

Punctuation marks are signals to the reader. They help make the message clearer.

Sometimes, the meaning of a sentence can change completely depending on the punctuation.

Punctuation Mark	Use	Examples
Period (.)	• To indicate the end of a complete sentence	• *My passion is singing.* • *He is an excellent artist.*
Comma (,)	• To separate items in a list • To separate two phrases • After introductory words	• *Please buy cheese, eggs, milk and bread.* • *Before you leave, please turn off the lights.* • *Dear John, I will do it tomorrow.* • *Tomorrow, it will be done.*
Question mark (?)	• To indicate a question	• *Where are you going?*
Exclamation mark (!)	• To indicate surprise or strong emotion	• *Wow! I can't believe you won!* • *That's fantastic!*
Apostrophe (')	• In contractions • To show possession	• *They **don't** want to take a taxi before seven **o'clock**.* • *Jane's phone number, the Smiths' address*
Colon (:)	• To introduce a list of items • In a business letter greeting • In time	• *This is what you need: a sleeping bag, a pillow, an extra blanket and warm clothes.* • *Dear Madam:* • *8:15 p.m.*
Semi-colon (;)	• To join related sentences into one sentence • For lists that already have commas in them	• *I told him not to go; it is too dangerous.* • *They toured: Toronto, ON; Montréal, QC; Halifax, NS and Moncton, NB.*
Hyphen (-)	• To make compound words • To write compound numbers • To join prefixes to words	• *Ghetto-blaster* • *Twenty-seven, seventy-seven* • *Mini-series, anti-social, semi-colon*
Parentheses ( )	• To give additional, non essential information	• *She thinks that Gabriel (who sits in front of me in French) is really cute.*
Quotation Marks (" ")	• To indicate a person's words	• *"Make yourself at home," she said.*

There is no comma after the next-to-last item.

There is no hyphen in New York, New Brunswick, etc.

⚠ PAY ATTENTION!

- **Commas and periods** always go **inside** the quotation marks.
- **Semi-colons and colons** always go **outside**.

- **Question marks** go inside if the question is part of the quotation and outside if it is not:
  "What is the answer?"
  Is the title, "Celluloid Heroes"?

126 Reference Section B   Thank you for not photocopying.   © Éditions Grand Duc

ACTIVITY 3

Insert the proper punctuation in the following text.

The Olympic Games

The Olympic Games which are held every four years are perhaps the world s most important athletic event Amateur athletes from every country compete in a variety of athletic events Each time the Games are held in a different city The Games were originally part of a religious ceremony to honour the Greek god Zeus Eventually the Games became the most important in all Greece and time was measured in the four-year periods between Games These periods were called Olympiads The first recorded Olympic Games were held in 776 BC the last ancient Olympic games were held in 393 AD when after 1 200 years of regularly held competitions Emperor Theodosius the First banned the Games

In the late 1800s a French archaeologist named Pierre de Coubertin revived the Games Through his efforts the first Olympiad of the modern era was held in Athens in 1896

ACTIVITY 4

Insert the appropriate punctuation marks in the following text.

A Historic Encounter

My friend Fred told the following anecdote about the song "Lady Madonna" by the Beatles It seems Fred was at the Anaconda Hotel in the very small village of Grand Heights when he ran into John Lennon who was vacationing incognito Fred being the music expert that he was recognized him right away He went up to him and said   John, what are you doing here   Of course John was very surprised   Who are you   he asked my friend in a somewhat annoyed tone Fred realizing his faux pas immediately extended his hand   My name is Fred and I am probably your biggest fan John still seemed annoyed   Listen my friend I am not who you think I am My name is Arthur Mellow   As Arthur or John turned to leave Fred exclaimed   That s right big shot turn your back on your fans   Arthur or John stopped turned around heaved a sigh and said   Okay you got me What can I do for you   Fred couldn't believe his ears John Lennon really wanted to know what he could do for him   Wow   thought Fred   It s the greatest day of my life   He thought for a minute and then slowly turned to John and asked   Where did you get the idea for the opening of 'All You Need Is Love'   John or Arthur smiled looked at Fred and whispered   It came from my friend Lady Madonna   With that he got into his rusted old car waved goodbye and left And that is how according to Fred the Beatles got the idea for the song "Lady Madonna"

Name: _____ Date: _____ Group: _____

REFERENCE SECTION C

Phrasal Verbs

A **phrasal verb** is composed of a **verb** and a **particle** (a **preposition**).

Adding this preposition to the verb gives a new meaning to the original verb.

Examples: To **look**: *to use the eyes to see.*
To **look after**: *to take care of someone, something.*
To **break**: *to make something come apart in pieces; smash, crack or split.*
To **break up**: *to end a relationship.*

Here is a list of common phrasal verbs:

Phrasal Verb (Verb + Particle)	Meaning
to **ask out**	to ask someone to go on a date
to **ask over**	to invite someone for a visit
to **break up**	to end a relationship
to **bring up**	to raise children, to mention a topic
to **call back**	to return a telephone call
to **call off**	to cancel
*to **call on**	to ask for someone's assistance for something
to **call up**	to make a telephone call
*to **catch up**	to reach the same position or level
to **check out**	to take a book from the library; to pay the bill and leave a hotel
to **cross out**	to draw a line through
to **do over**	to do again
*to **drop out**	to quit school or classes
to **figure out**	to find the solution to a problem
to **fill in**	to complete a sentence by writing in a blank
to **fill out**	to write information on a form
to **fill up**	to fill completely with gas, water, coffee, etc.
to **find out**	to discover information
to **get along**	to have a good relationship
to **get in**	to enter a car, a taxi
*to **get off**	to leave a bus, airplane, train or subway, or dismount from a bicycle
*to **get on**	to enter a bus, airplane, train or subway, or mount a bicycle

*These phrasal verbs are inseparable; the object of the verb must appear after the particle.

Phrasal Verb (Verb + Particle)	Meaning
*to **get over**	to recover from a bad situation (marks, dates, disputes, etc.)
to **give up**	to quit doing something or quit trying
to **grow up**	to become an adult
to **hand in**	to give homework, tests, papers, etc., to a teacher
to **hand out**	to distribute something, usually to a group of people
to **hang up**	to end a telephone call
to **keep up**	to continue; to maintain
to **leave out**	to omit or exclude
*to **look after**	to take care of something or somebody
to **look up**	to search for information in a reference book
to **make up**	to invent; to patch up an argument
*to **pass away**	to die
to **pick up**	to lift
to **put away**	to put something in its usual or proper place
to **put back**	to return something to its original place
to **put down**	to stop holding or carrying something
to **put off**	to postpone or delay
to **put on**	to dress
to **put out**	to extinguish (stop) a fire, a cigarette, a cigar
to **put up with**	to tolerate
*to **run into**	to meet someone by chance
to **shut off**	to stop a machine or turn off a light
to **start over**	to start again from the beginning
*to **take after**	to resemble
to **take off**	to remove something, to undress; to leave
to **take up**	to start a new activity
to **tear down**	to destroy a structure, like a building
to **tear off**	to detach something; tear along a dotted or perforated line
to **tear up**	to tear into small pieces
to **throw away/out**	to put in the trash
to **try on**	to put on clothing to see if it fits
to **turn down**	to decrease the volume; decline an offer
to **turn off**	to stop a machine or shut off a light
to **turn on**	to start a machine or flick on a light
to **turn up**	to increase the volume; to appear somewhere
to **write down**	to write a note on a piece of paper

*These phrasal verbs are inseparable; the object of the verb must appear after the particle.

REFERENCE SECTION D

Idiomatic Expressions (Idioms)

Idioms are expressions often linked to an image that is used to express something figuratively. Here are a few common idiomatic expressions:

Idiom	Meaning
all in your head	imaginary, not real
all that jazz	everything similar or related
bad hair day	things not going the way you would like
bag of bones	someone is very underweight
below par	not doing very well, below average
brain like a sieve	to have a bad memory or be very forgetful
by the skin of your teeth	to only just manage to do something and come very close to failing
elbow grease	hard physical work
fit as a fiddle	perfect health
heads up	advance information or warning
hook, line and sinker	completely
it takes two to tango	when things go wrong, both sides are involved and not completely innocent
light years ahead	a long way in front of others
no skin off my nose	something that doesn't affect or bother you
not rocket science	not difficult to understand
on your toes	alert and ready to go
out of hand	out of control
rule of thumb	approximately
to be all ears	to be very interested in hearing about something
to bite your tongue	to refrain from speaking
to call the tune	to make important decisions
to cost an arm and a leg	to be very expensive
to cover all the bases	to deal with or anticipate all possibilities
to get your feet wet	to experience something for the first time
to live to tell the tale	to survive a terrible experience
to throw caution to the wind	to stop caring about the possible dangers and start taking risks
to toot your own horn	to boast about your own achievement

Name: _____ Date: _____ Group: _____

ACTIVITY 5

Choose the phrasal verb that best fits the underlined expression.

a) The breakup was very hard but he is slowly underlined{recovering}. _____

b) Due to a lack of ticket sales, they underlined{cancelled} the concert. _____

c) You'll never guess who I underlined{met} at the market today. _____

d) Do whatever you want. underlined{It doesn't bother me at all}. _____

e) I have underlined{tolerated} your insubordination long enough. _____

ACTIVITY 6

Write the idiomatic expression represented by the following illustrations.

Answer: _____

Answer: _____

Answer: _____

Answer: _____

Answer: _____

Answer: _____

Answer: _____

Answer: _____

Answer: _____

© Éditions Grand Duc   Thank you for not photocopying.   Reference Section D   131

REFERENCE SECTION E

An Overview of Verb Tenses

Here is a table explaining the main verb tenses used in English:

Tense	When to Use It	How to Form It	Examples
Simple past	• For an action that finished sometime in the past	Add **-d**, **-ed** or **-ied** to the base form of regular verbs.	• I **lost** my cellphone this morning. • My brother **bought** a new car yesterday. • We **didn't see** the program. • She **didn't have** time to finish.
Past continuous	• For an action that was going on in the past when something interrupted it • For two simultaneous actions	Past of *to be* **(was/were)** + base form + **ing**	• She **was playing** the trumpet when the announcement came. • We **were eating** supper when he got the news. • She **was talking** on the phone while she **was eating**.
Past perfect	• For an action in the past that happened before another one	**had** + past participle	• They **had** already **left** when Marina arrived. • I **had left** before you called.
Present perfect	• For an action that is finished but that has a direct link with the present. There is more action to come.	**have (has)** + past participle	• The family **has visited** France many times. • Romano **has learned** to speak French very well.
Simple present	• For habits or usual activities • For facts • For likes and dislikes	Base form of the verb (*Third person singular always ends in "s."*)	• I **take** piano lessons every week. • We **don't understand**. • Madrid **is** the capital of Spain. • He **lives** in Toronto now. • He **doesn't go** there after work.
Present continuous	• For an action that is happening right now • For an action that will happen in the near future • For irritations (with *always*)	Present of *to be* **(am, is, are)** + base form + **ing**	• Mark **is planning** a surprise party for Karina. • We **are taking** a trip in June. • Julianna **isn't attending** the party. • Telemarketers **are** always **calling** us at suppertime.
Future	• For an action in the future • To express a future intention • To make predictions	**will** + base form	• I **will travel** to Australia when I have enough money. • I **won't forget** to call your mother. • The Black Hawks **will win**.
Future continuous	• For an action that will be taking place in the future	**will be** + base form + **ing**	• Anita **will be playing** goalie tomorrow.
Conditional	• For an action that is hypothetical • For an action that will happen only under certain circumstances	**would** + base form	• I **would go**, too, but I am sick. • They **would like** to live in Mexico. • Jack **would love** to own a Porsche.

How to Form the Negative Form of Verbs:

Verb Tense	Auxiliary	Verb Form	Examples
Simple present	do not/does not don't/doesn't	+ base form	• I **don't know**. • He **doesn't care**.
Simple past	did not/didn't	+ base form	• They **didn't come**.
Future	will not/won't	+ base form	• We **won't go** there.
Present continuous	am not/is not are not/isn't aren't	+ base form + ing	• I'm **not reading**.
Past continuous	was not/were not wasn't/weren't	+ base form + ing	• They **were not talking**. • Linda **wasn't chewing** gum.
Future continuous	will not be/won't be	+ base form + ing	• She **will not be visiting** her cousin next summer.
Present perfect	have not/has not haven't/hasn't	+ past participle	• She **has not seen** them. • You **haven't been** there.
Past perfect	had not/hadn't	+ past participle	• Barbara **hadn't seen** him.
Conditional	would not/wouldn't	+ base form	• I **wouldn't go** there.

How to Form the Interrogative Form of Verbs:

Verb Tense	Auxiliary	Verb Form	Examples
Simple present	do/does	+ base form	**Does** he **live** in the city?
Simple past	did	+ base form	**Did** he **go** to the store?
Future	will	+ base form	**Will** he **study** after school?
Present continuous	am/are/is	+ base form + ing	**Is** he **going** to the party?
Past continuous	was/were	+ base form + ing	**Was** he **going** home?
Future continuous	will be	+ base form + ing	**Will** we **be singing** at the festival?
Present perfect	have/has	+ past participle	**Has** he **left** yet?
Past perfect	had	+ past participle	**Had** he **received** a gift?
Conditional	would	+ base form	**Would** he **come** with us?

How to Form a Question with a Question Word:

Question Word	Auxiliary	Subject	Verb	Rest of the Question
Where	does	Rosie	go	skiing?
Why	has	he	decided	to buy a pickup truck?
When	will	they	record	a new CD?

Reference Section E

ACTIVITY 7

Write the verbs in parentheses in the appropriate verb tense with the help of the highlighted markers.

Predictable...

John always (to follow) _____ the same routine every morning. He (to get) _____ up at 6 a.m., (to put) _____ on a pot of coffee and (to go) _____ outside to get the newspaper from the mailbox. He (to read) _____ the paper while he (to drink) _____ his coffee. After that, he (to take) _____ a shower, (to dress) _____ and then (to brush) _____ his teeth. At precisely 7:10, he (to leave) _____ the house and (to drive) _____ to work. It's always the same routine.

I (to ask) _____ John to change his routine many times. Today, he finally (to do) _____ it, but not on purpose...

Usually, John (to get) _____ up at 6 a.m., but this morning he (get up, neg.) _____ until 7. His alarm clock (to ring, neg.) _____. He (to jump) _____ out of bed. He (to take) _____ a quick shower, but there (to be) _____ no time to shave or read the paper. He (to leave) _____ it in the mailbox. He (to grab) _____ his coat and a cold cup of coffee and (to run) _____ out the door. He (to be) _____ in such a hurry that he (to miss) _____ a stop. However, the policeman (to miss, neg.) _____ him.

When John (to arrive) _____ at the corner, he (to drink) _____ his cold coffee and (to see, neg.) _____ the police car. He (to try) _____ to explain to the police officer that he (to be) _____ simply distracted and that he had not noticed the stop. The officer (to smile) _____, (to say) _____ he (to understand) _____ and (to give) _____ him a ticket anyway. He (to think) _____ about the ticket when he (to drive) _____ forward and (to forget) _____ that the police cruiser (to be) _____ right in front of him. Guess what? He drove right into it!

I'm sure that on the way back from work this evening, he (to stop) _____ and he (to buy) _____ a couple of batteries. I'm also sure he (to be) _____ back to his old routine tomorrow morning.

134 Reference Section E

Name: _____ Date: _____ Group: _____

ACTIVITY 8

Write the following sentences in the interrogative form, as indicated.

Example: It rained very hard last Saturday.

    a) Yes/No question: Did it rain very hard last Saturday?

    b) Information question: When did it rain very hard? **or** How did it rain last Saturday? **or** What happened last Saturday?

1. She is reading a very good novel at the moment.

    a) Y/N Q: _____

    b) Info Q: _____

2. They left for the Himalayas last weekend.

    a) Y/N Q: _____

    b) Info Q: _____

3. He practises many sports during the year.

    a) Y/N Q: _____

    b) Info Q: _____

4. They were swimming in the lake when the storm arose.

    a) Y/N Q: _____

    b) Info Q: _____

5. She has done that work many times before.

    a) Y/N Q: _____

    b) Info Q: _____

6. They had already seen that movie when she invited them.

    a) Y/N Q: _____

    b) Info Q: _____

7. They will arrive on Friday by train.

    a) Y/N Q: _____

    b) Info Q: _____

8. He would buy a new car if he had the money.

    a) Y/N Q: _____

    b) Info Q: _____

Reference Section E

ACTIVITY 9

Write the following sentences in the negative form.

a) They always arrive at practice on time.
_____

b) She has already learned that piece by heart.
_____

c) They were rafting in Colorado when they got the news.
_____

d) I have visited Machu Picchu several times already.
_____

e) James had a huge heart tattooed on his chest.
_____

f) The journalist is interviewing the witnesses to the accident.
_____

g) They will compete in the next winter Olympics.
_____

h) He wrote his last musical comedy before he left the country.
_____

i) Sarah believes that everything has a purpose in life.
_____

j) They are presently reading all they need to know about mountain climbing.
_____

ACTIVITY 10

Underline the verbs in the following sentences and identify the verb tenses.

a) I wrote an email to my friend last night.   _____

b) My grandparents have lived in the same house
   for the past 50 years.   _____

c) She was working on her text when her computer broke down.   _____

d) If he ran for office, he would surely be elected.   _____

e) I can't talk right now, I'm working.   _____

f) My daughter will graduate in three years.   _____

g) Everyday, we eat the same thing for lunch.   _____

h) He had finished writing his novel when he lost the manuscript.   _____

Reference Section E

ACTIVITY 11

Write the verbs in parentheses in the appropriate tense.

A Trip to Peru

Our last trip to South America (to start) _____ on a cold March day. We (to prepare) _____ for this adventure many months before. We all (to know) _____ it (to be) _____ different than what we were used to, but how different was yet to be discovered. Things (to go) _____ smoothly from the start. Our bus (to come) _____ to pick us up at school as scheduled. The driver (to be) _____ experienced, so we (to know) _____ we (to get) _____ to the airport on time. And we (to do) _____. At the airport, things were not as smooth. Everyone was nervous. We suddenly (to realize) _____ that we (to leave) _____ our country and (to be) _____ on our way to a foreign country we (to know, neg.) _____ much about. The person in charge of the group (to gather) _____ the students around her and (to give) _____ us a last-minute talk before we (to board) _____ the plane. She (to say) _____, "You (to see) _____ many wonderful things on this trip. We (to visit) _____ places you (to read, only) _____ about in books. We (to work, also) _____ in a vineyard for a while so you (to understand) _____ the hardships those people (to endure) _____ every day just to make a living. There (to be) _____ rules to follow. The most important (to be) _____ this: we always (to remain) _____ in a group. If you (to get) _____ lost, (to stay) _____ where you are: we (to find) _____ you. Once we (to arrive) _____ in Peru, our guide (to meet) _____ us at the airport. He (to be) _____ an excellent guide who (to know) _____ everything there is to know about the places we (to visit) _____."

Our guide (to meet) _____ us at our arrival and quickly (to take) _____ control of the group. A bus (to wait) _____ for us as we (to leave) _____ the terminal. The first thing we (to notice) _____ was the heat; we (to leave) _____ in the cold of winter and (to arrive) _____ in the heat of summer. To make a long story short, we (to visit) _____ four cities and Machu Picchu. The second leg of our trip (to take) _____ us further south to Argentina, where we (to work) _____ for a week in a vineyard in the region of Mendoza. Some of us soon (to realize) _____ that we (to complain) _____ on a full stomach all our lives. One of the boys (to remark) _____, "I realize now that I (to be, always) _____ a bit self-centred. This experience (to open) _____ my eyes."

It (to open) _____ many eyes!

Name: _____ Date: _____ Group: _____

REFERENCE SECTION F

Table of Common Irregular Verbs

Use this colour code to highlight or colour the table of irregular verbs. You already have four examples at the beginning of the table.

Colour code	Examples
A - A - A	bet - bet - bet
A - B - A	become - became - become
A - B - B	bend - bent - bent
A - B - C	awake - awoke - awoken

Base Form	Simple Past	Past Participle	Base Form	Simple Past	Past Participle
arise	arose	arisen	clothe	clothed/clad	clothed/clad
awake	awoke	awoken	come	came	come
babysit	babysat	babysat	cost	cost	cost
be	was/were	been	creep	crept	crept
bear	bore	borne	cut	cut	cut
beat	beat	beaten	deal	dealt	dealt
become	became	become	dig	dug	dug
begin	began	begun	dive	dove	dived
bend	bent	bent	do	did	done
bet	bet	bet	draw	drew	drawn
bid	bid	bid	dream	dreamed/dreamt	dreamed/dreamt
bind	bound	bound	drink	drank	drunk
bite	bit	bitten	drive	drove	driven
bleed	bled	bled	eat	ate	eaten
blow	blew	blown	fall	fell	fallen
break	broke	broken	feed	fed	fed
breed	bred	bred	feel	felt	felt
bring	brought	brought	fight	fought	fought
build	built	built	find	found	found
burn	burned/burnt	burned/burnt	fit	fit	fit
burst	burst	burst	flee	fled	fled
bust	bust/busted	bust/busted	fly	flew	flown
buy	bought	bought	forbid	forbade	forbidden
cast	cast	cast	forecast	forecast	forecast
catch	caught	caught	foresee	foresaw	foreseen
choose	chose	chosen	foretell	foretold	foretold
cling	clung	clung	forget	forgot	forgotten

Reference Section F — Thank you for not photocopying. — © Éditions Grand Duc

Base Form	Simple Past	Past Participle	Base Form	Simple Past	Past Participle
forgive	forgave	forgiven	outdo	outdid	outdone
forsake	forsook	forsaken	overcome	overcame	overcome
freeze	froze	frozen	overdo	overdid	overdone
get	got	gotten	overeat	overate	overeaten
give	gave	given	overhear	overheard	overheard
go	went	gone	overlay	overlaid	overlain
grind	ground	ground	overpay	overpaid	overpaid
grow	grew	grown	overrun	overran	overrun
handwrite	handwrote	handwritten	oversleep	overslept	overslept
hang	hung	hung	overtake	overtook	overtaken
have	had	had	partake	partook	partaken
hear	heard	heard	pay	paid	paid
hide	hid	hid	plead	pleaded/pled	pleaded/pled
hold	held	held	prepay	prepaid	prepaid
hurt	hurt	hurt	preshrink	preshrank	preshrunk
keep	kept	kept	proofread	proofread	proofread
kneel	knelt/kneeled	knelt/kneeled	prove	proved	proven
knit	knit/knitted	knit/knitted	put	put	put
know	knew	known	quit	quit	quit
lay	laid	laid	read	read	read
lead	led	led	rebuild	rebuilt	rebuilt
lean	leaned/leant	leaned/leant	remake	remade	remade
leap	leaped/leapt	leaped/leapt	repay	repaid	repaid
learn	learned/learnt	learned/learnt	rerun	reran	rerun
leave	left	left	resell	resold	resold
lend	lent	lent	retell	retold	retold
let	let	let	rewind	rewound	rewound
lie	lay	lain	ride	rode	ridden
light	lit/lighted	lit/lighted	ring	rang	rung
lose	lost	lost	rise	rose	risen
make	made	made	run	ran	run
mean	meant	meant	saw	sawed	sawed/sawn
meet	met	met	say	said	said
mislay	mislaid	mislaid	see	saw	seen
misread	misread	misread	seek	sought	sought
mistake	mistook	mistaken	sell	sold	sold
misunderstand	misunderstood	misunderstood	send	sent	sent
mow	mowed	mown	set	set	set

Reference Section F 139

Name: _____ Date: _____ Group: _____

Base Form	Simple Past	Past Participle	Base Form	Simple Past	Past Participle
sew	sewed	sewed/sewn	strike	struck	stricken
shake	shook	shaken	string	strung	strung
shave	shaved	shaved/shaven	strive	strove	striven
shear	sheared	shorn	swear	swore	sworn
shed	shed	shed	sweat	sweat/sweated	sweat/sweated
shine	shone/shined	shone/shined	sweep	swept	swept
shoot	shot	shot	swell	swelled	swollen/swelled
show	showed	shown	swim	swam	swum
shrink	shrank	shrunk	swing	swung	swung
shut	shut	shut	take	took	taken
sing	sang	sung	teach	taught	taught
sink	sank	sunk	tear	tore	torn
sit	sat	sat	telecast	telecast	telecast
slay	slew	slain	tell	told	told
sleep	slept	slept	think	thought	thought
slide	slid	slid	throw	threw	thrown
sling	slung	slung	thrust	thrust	thrust
slink	slunk	slunk	tread	trod	trodden/trod
slit	slit	slit	underfeed	underfed	underfed
smell	smelled/smelt	smelled/smelt	undergo	underwent	undergone
sneak	sneaked/snuck	sneaked/snuck	understand	understood	understood
sow	sowed	sown	undertake	undertook	undertaken
speak	spoke	spoken	undo	undid	undone
speed	sped	sped	unwind	unwound	unwound
spell	spelled/spelt	spelled/spelt	uphold	upheld	upheld
spend	spent	spent	upset	upset	upset
spill	spilled/spilt	spilled/spilt	wake	woke	waken
spin	spun	spun	wear	wore	worn
spit	spit/spat	spit/spat	weave	weaved/wove	weaved/woven
split	split	split	wed	wed/wedded	wed/wedded
spread	spread	spread	weep	wept	wept
spring	sprang/sprung	sprang/sprung	win	won	won
stand	stood	stood	wind	wound	wound
steal	stole	stolen	withdraw	withdrew	withdrawn
stick	stuck	stuck	withhold	withheld	withheld
sting	stung	stung	withstand	withstood	withstood
stink	stank	stunk	wring	wrung	wrung
			write	wrote	written

Reference Section F